THE LANG
OF FLOW

 a beginner's guide

THE LANGUAGE
OF FLOWERS
 a beginner's guide

KRISTYNA ARCARTI

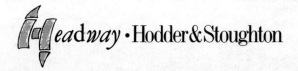

A catalogue record for this title is available from the British Library.

ISBN 0 340 69781 4

First published 1997
Impression number 10 9 8 7 6 5 4 3 2 1
Year   2001 2000 1999 1998 1997

Typeset by Transet Limited, Coventry, England.
Printed in Great Britain for Hodder & Stoughton Educational, a division of Hodder Headline plc, 338 Euston Road, London NW1 3BH by Cox and Wyman Limited, Reading, Berks.

To my parents to whom I owe everything I am
and everything I have become

CONTENTS

INTRODUCTION

When we look at the world around us, we cannot fail to be impressed by the power and beauty of nature. We only have to think of the varieties of species of flora and fauna to realise how much there is out there. In this book I will try to help you discover the world of flowers and how they have been used in the past and can be used in the present.

This is not a gardening book, however – we are not going to talk about planning a garden, what types of flowers come into bloom when, or anything related to horticulture. If you are interested in astrology you may be interested to learn that there are special times at which plants are best tended. Magazines are currently available which provide such information for the amateur lunar gardener. Gardening and flowers can and do mean different things to different people. Those people with a love of gardening will think there's nothing better than to spend time in the garden, growing seedlings, planting out, tending to their gardens. On the other hand, those people who have little time, dislike gardening but can appreciate the benefits of a garden will perhaps not wish to bother about learning the art of garden maintenance. Aware of these dichotomies, I have tried in this book to give as much information as possible, within the space available, on plants and herbs and their use in the home and as gifts, rather than spend time discussing what to plant, where to plant it and what the best avenues are for the amateur gardener, or giving detailed information on how to arrange plants and flowers around the home. These topics can easily fill a book on their own, so this is merely a stepping stone to further study.

While I actively appreciate flowers, and take great delight in the wonderful gardens that abound, I am certainly no gardener. What I am going to do is take a detailed look at flowers, investigating their meaning and the superstitions associated with some of them. We will concentrate mainly on what other people have felt about flowers. We will look at folklore, at other people's views on the meaning of flowers and herbs, flower symbolism and names, and the use of colour.

Every year, millions of people will wear a poppy in November as a symbol of remembrance. Do we really know when and why this tradition evolved? There are other traditional usages of flowers and plants, for example kissing under the mistletoe at Christmas. Why are roses associated with romance, and why do we think in terms of red roses to signify passion and love? During the course of this book, we are going to discover why these traditions have developed, delve into myths and legends, then bring it all bang up to date.

Many people give flowers to loved ones at times of birthdays, anniversaries and so on. We also give flowers to people when they are ill, knowing instinctively that the blooms will help to cheer up the person concerned. We send flowers as an expression of sympathy at funerals. We may seek out various flowers to plant in our gardens, not only because of the colours they have, but often for more deep-seated reasons, and likewise, we also dismiss certain flowers because we don't feel comfortable with them owing to a superstitious connotation. For example, when I was a child, my mother never allowed me to bring lilac into the house. It was unlucky she said, especially white lilac which invited death into the household. This possibly stems from the age-old belief that any heavily scented flower was the home of dead souls and that whiteness was linked to death. Another superstition which my mother acted upon was the mixing of red and white flowers. This, she said, was a big 'No' because it resembled blood and bandages, and as a result, should never be given in a bouquet, especially to someone who was ill or in hospital. The periwinkle, a lovely blue flower which can be found in many gardens, is called *Fiore di morte* by the Italians and is used to make garlands for dead babies, so has come to be associated with death and the dead. Many people, aware of this superstition, will not have periwinkles in their gardens.

Even though such superstitions are highly irrational in the most part, especially in the age of technology in which we live, the discovery of their origins and meanings can uncover many hidden fears and desires which we would otherwise seek to subdue.

Throughout this book, we will be looking at many superstitions, both current and age-old, examining various esoteric linkages, and also investigating the symbolism of flowers, both from the Victorian standpoint and in current thought, as well as looking at gardens of past and present.

We owe a lot more to the world of flowers and plants than we are able to cover in this book. Flowers and plants have always been used for medicinal purposes, in homoeopathy, aromatherapy, herbalism and meditation, but I must leave this for another book in this series.

Enjoy your flowers, plants, herbs and gardens. In the changing face of the world, your garden may be the only place where you can go to relax, and the giving and receiving of flowers will always be a special bond between individuals, irrespective of the world outside.

bistorical uses of flowers and plants

In this chapter, we are going to take a step back in time, and look at historical gardens, the use of flowers and plants in rituals and what giving plants and flowers meant in times gone by and folklore. Some of these traditions still continue, and others, although hidden from our conscious minds, are things with which we can link, even in our modern technological age. We will also see how people have sought to create a paradise area for relaxation and peace of mind.

Our Love of the garden and flowers

Most of us, even if we dislike gardening, can appreciate a lovely garden, and flowers and plants. We may not understand them, how they grow, when to plant them, and what they need to survive, but we can all enjoy the beauty of a well-kept garden and find tranquillity within it. We might not have the time or facilities to create or tend a garden of our own, but we all can benefit from gardens and parklands.

Today, most of us lead hectic lives, and need somewhere quiet, perhaps with lawns, flowers, trees and ponds where we can relax. You can often see office workers in the parks at lunchtimes during the summer, just lying or sitting there, taking the time to relax and unwind. It is good to relax in our own garden or in a local park where we can have a picnic or walk with our families and friends.

Many people visit Kew Gardens in Britain. Others travel to gardens in France, at Versailles for example, in Japan at Kyoto, or in the United States in Longwood, Pennsylvania.

Many people love gardens and gardening. One such was the US president Thomas Jefferson, who was devoted to gardening, and even in his advancing years claimed that he was 'but a young gardener'.

Scientists claim that when we are in touch with the world of nature, we are happier as a result, and our health improves. Indeed, there are many who feel that we are nearer to God in a garden than anywhere else on earth. There is a little sign in a garden area near to my home which says just that, and I often feel that a visit to that place brings about a more tranquil state of mind. Many hospitals now have gardens where their patients can sit, and even in New York City one hospital has planted a garden on its roof for the benefit of its patients.

GARDENS OF THE PAST

The Hanging Gardens of Babylon are known to most of us, although we may all have totally differing views as to what they actually looked like, as nobody truly knows. They were built by King Nebuchadnezzar for his Median wife over 2,500 years ago. The king wanted to create an area of forests and hills to make his wife less homesick for her native land. The 23-metre (75-foot high) stepped structure of arched vaults, all richly planted, contained enough soil to nurture large trees, and it is possible that there were waterfalls, mosaic walkways and planted areas as well.

In Egyptian times, landscaping was widespread, and the discovery of a landscape plan of a garden belonging to an Egyptian official at Thebes, dating from about 1400 BCE shows ponds, tree-lined avenues and pavilions. Most royal gardens had flower groves, herbs and ponds, and possibly also lakes.

It is thought that the gardens of Persia were also stunning. Alexander the Great returned to Greece in the fourth century BCE from the area, bringing with him seeds, plants and many ideas for landscaping.

Persian gardens seemed to the Arabs in particular to be representative of the paradise promised to the faithful in the Koran, and as such, the typical Arab garden was normally split into four sections by four streams, linked at the centre by a pool or a fountain.

In Athens, Aristotle and Theophrastus, his pupil, put together many inventories of flora, and established a botanical garden in which they could study and classify plants. Indeed, many wealthy Greeks had beautiful gardens, and it is recorded that the temples to the gods were lovely areas, with both an abundance of flora and fauna, where considerable use was made of water and its natural peace-giving properties.

The Romans were also very fond of their gardens. Beautiful areas were considered of paramount importance, and it is said that Nero ruthlessly evicted hundreds of families from their homes, which he subsequently demolished, to create a private park of over 125 acres around his palace. Later, about CE 138, Emperor Hadrian had 600 acres of parks, pools, lakes and fountains surrounding his villa.

The ancient Israelites, too, had gardens and parks, and historian Josephus talks about park areas with streams at a place called Etam, which was around 16 km (10 miles) outside Jerusalem. In the Bible there are accounts of the Mount of Olives, the Garden of Gethsemane and other such beautiful areas.

In China it was felt that rivers, rocks and mountains were all materialised spirits, and so garden areas were respected, leading to many gardens following Taoist, Confucianist and Buddhist designs. Japanese gardens, however, developed along slightly differing lines, with precision being more important than colour. This resulted in the art of bonsai, which actually means 'potted plant', where a miniature tree is trained into a specific form and proportion. Space being limited in Japan, bonsai became very popular, and indeed still is, not only in Japan but throughout the world. Water areas are also essential parts of garden design in Japan, in an attempt to provide utmost tranquillity.

Many other cultures such as the Aztecs and Incas have sought to create beautiful garden areas. It is said that the seventeenth-century Mogul rulers of northern India planted more than 700 beautiful

gardens, forming a blaze of colour, sprinkled with fountains, terraces and cascades. The black marble pavilion built on Lake Dal's shore by the builder of the Taj Mahal still carries the inscription 'If there is a paradise on the face of the earth, it is here'.

Nearer to modern times, the gardens of the Palace of Versailles, built by King Louis XIV, display the grandeur of Renaissance landscaping with its geometric designs, and the clipping and shaping of trees and shrubs, known to us as topiary. Topiary was not a new form, but something resurrected from Roman times. Following the Renaissance, and especially with the increase in trade and exploration around the world, many countries enjoyed a flourishing period of garden design. In Britain well-known landscape designers such as William Kent and Lancelot Brown were used by those wealthy enough to employ their talents, and it is said that Brown laid out more than 200 estates. Indeed US presidents John Adams and Thomas Jefferson came to England in 1786 to study English gardens.

Use oF FLOWERS aND pLANTS IN RITUALS

The Greek god of healing, Asclepius, in whose honour temples were erected, had various scented posies offered to him, while those flowers offered to Aphrodite, goddess of love, were said to have aphrodisiac qualities.

In many lands, plants were considered sacred to the gods. In northern India, for example, the *Rig-Veda*, a sacred book of knowledge, carried with it details of a god-plant, known as *soma*. The plant would undergo a ritual preparation and was then transported to a place of sacrifice, where it would be soaked with water drawn especially for the purpose, before being squeezed between pressing stones. The liquid which resulted was then mixed with milk or with honey and strained through woollen strainers. This liquid was sprinkled on the altar on which a sacrifice was to be made, as well as being placed on the grass in front of where it was thought

the attending gods would sit. Various theories as to what the soma actually was have been passed down to us; it is possible that soma was, in fact, the red-capped toadstool (the sort of toadstool which became a common illustration in Victorian children's story books).

Many gods were associated with plants and flowers. In Roman times, the god of wine, Bacchus, had as his plant the ivy. It was, at one time, fashionable for taverns and wine shops to be marked by an ivy plant or garland, as a sign that wine was on sale within. Bacchus was often portrayed with a garland of ivy around his head, and in Roman times it is said that worshippers of Bacchus would chew ivy in order to get themselves into a 'magical' state. It was also thought that if a priest of Jupiter touched an ivy plant he would be put into a prophetic state of mind. Likewise, the Romans also used the laurel leaf, symbolising victory, to give to victors of battles and to those who won in athletic events. It is said that Emperor Tiberius was so afraid of thunderstorms that he always wore a crown of laurel during a storm, crawling under his bed for added protection. The Romans felt that the laurel would protect them against evil, and it is interesting today to note how many houses, where laurels do not feature within the garden, are called 'The Laurels', possibly for similar reasons.

Within what is called the 'old tradition', otherwise known as paganism or Wicca, are many uses of flowers and herbs – not surprising when one considers that a love of nature is fundamental to pagan beliefs. Amongst the magical correspondences (that is, the linking of certain things for ritual workings) are not only flowers but also herbs, stones and animals, which are associated with various gods and goddesses. For example, for matters of love and happiness, rose, thyme and mint might be considered appropriate. Concerns of home and family are addressed by the use of jasmine, lotus, willow and gardenia. Matters of health and protection employ orange, carnation and rosemary, while to strengthen communication and self-improvement lavender, fennel and dill are used. Those in need of courage or strength can use coriander and basil, while prosperity and settlement of legal problems utilise sage, honeysuckle and clover. If it is felt that a centring is necessary, because of a need to bind together or protect, comfrey, pansy and yew might be considered.

You can find out more about correspondences in two other books in this series – *Witchcraft – a beginner's guide* and *Paganism – a beginner's guide*. Many of these correspondences are still used: flowers decorate Christian churches, and at times, such as Harvest Festival, other plants, and vegetables, fruits and wild flowers are placed on and around the altar. The original pagan tradition of linking flowers, fragrances and candles is especially noteworthy, as perfumed candles and flowers are correspondences used to mark important celebrations.

Earth magic and predictions

As we have seen, many peoples over the centuries have practised magical rituals using the power of nature. Many also believe that trees, plants and even the soil can be used to help us in our lives.

An esoteric artform known as earth magic, which uses the four elements of air, earth, fire and water, uses soil in rituals. Believing, for example, that placing a saucer of fresh earth in your room will combat illness, students of earth magic explain that the earth emits certain vibrations which help to assist in the recovery processes. Soil can be used to protect against anxieties, according to some beliefs. People take soil with them in a handkerchief and keep it in their pockets, feeling that it will give them extra confidence, especially when travelling overseas or away from their home base.

Students of earth magic feel that certain flowers and plants will help with certain areas of life, and that taking a seed and speaking to the seed about the problem before planting will help in this respect. If there are problems in relationships, jasmine and meadowsweet are thought to help. Problems with money require the help of camomile and honeysuckle, while peonies and snapdragons will help to protect and keep one safe.

Predictions and floramancy

Floramancy is an ancient esoteric form which uses all sorts of flowers and plants in prediction rituals. As we have already seen in

this chapter, many peoples over the centuries have used flowers in order to achieve love, and we may all at some time or another have blown at a dandelion and counted the number of puffs it takes to remove all the seeds, which is said to reveal the number of years before you marry. Likewise, we may all at some time have removed the petals from a daisy, and recited 'he/she loves me, he/she loves me not'.

Floramancy is quite a detailed form in its own right, but if you wish to find out how many children you will have, you might like to try this experiment, but don't necessarily hold the answer you receive as fast and true! Take the yellow centre from a daisy, roll it between your fingers, and then toss the particles from the bottom of your palm towards the fingers. It is said that the number of pieces which remain in your hand will be the number of children you will have. Students of palmistry might have other ideas here!

GiViNG aNd usiNG fLOWERS iN BYGONE DaYS

Upon the death of a person, many people will send either a flower basket or spray, or possibly a wreath, and it is worth noting that the placing of wreaths and flowers as a means of remembrance and, indeed, of reverence goes way back to our earliest history. Tradition tells us that floral wreaths originally were intended to enclose the soul of the loved one, and prevent it coming back to haunt the living. If you look at illustrations of Roman emperors and gods, many, if not all, will have upon their heads wreaths or crowns made of flowers and plants. Linking flowers with the concept of the circle, being an infinite entity in its own right, and feeling that circles contained magical powers, many Romans knew of the powerful effect this could have.

Not only Roman emperors and gods wore floral crowns – it is said that in ancient Peru, the maidens consecrated to the temples of the sun god wore crowns of sunflowers, quite appropriately. In ancient Greece, many people wore garlands of flowers, and the tradition of bedecking three-year-old children with flowers at the celebrations of

the Spring Equinox showed the recognition of their reaching childhood safely without illness, which robbed many families of their infants. Sadly many children died early on in their lives, and in certain parts of what is now Germany children who wore flowers before their first birthday were said to be certain to die, while in Switzerland the customs of crowning children with the crocus flower was said to help ward off evil and illness.

Biblical stories in the Hebrew scriptures concerning the use of garlands almost always refer to pagan practices, with accounts of drunkards wearing garlands of flowers on their heads during drinking sessions. And in the Greek scriptures, priests of Zeus are recorded as bringing bulls and garlands to the city gates to offer as sacrifices. Such garlands were usually made up of flowers and plants likely to be pleasing to whichever god was being worshipped. Various gods and goddesses in ancient times were associated with particular flowers and plants. In England, for example, those who worshipped the moon goddess would have had great respect for the elder wood, which was commonly known as lady wood, because the blossoms resembled the roundness of the moon. Many cultures and civilisations linked plants, trees and flowers with their gods. Worshippers of the gods would bring flowers in baskets or made into garlands or wreaths and place these at the temples, leaving them to wither and fade before being removed. Many religions still actively use garlands as tributes to their gods, the Hindu faith being just one of these; and in ancient Mexico it is recorded that plants, for example laurel, were used as sacrificial implements on the altars.

Only certain people were allowed to wear garlands of flowers in public. One such case was those who had saved the life of a person, when the wreath of green oak was given. Such people held high status in Rome, and when they walked into the room, everybody without exception was expected to rise to their feet. Possibly as a direct result of the increased wearing of garlands by mere mortals, the Romans eventually passed a law directing punishment for breaches of 'indiscriminate wearing of garlands'. It is said that one man was imprisoned for 16 years because he wore a garland of roses, while another was put in chains for crowning himself with flowers which had been acquired from a statue of Mersyas.

11

The poppy was associated with Ceres, and the sunflower with sun gods. Poppies were considered to be sacred to Ares, the Greek god of war, possibly due to their red colour being symbolic of blood, and therefore they were said to evoke bravery. The goddess Venus, connected strongly with love and passion, had as her flower the anemone, which as we will learn later has associations other than love to certain peoples. Lilies were associated with Hera, goddess of marriage and were famous within the poems of Homer, and were also used in Jewish history as a means of protection against witchcraft. Myrtle is associated with Artemis, virgin goddess of the chase and a moon goddess. Lilies, incidentally, with their white colour, are often seen to symbolise purity, and their link with the goddess of marriage should not surprise us. Likewise, in British history, we can read the account of John Aubrey who wrote, in 1686, of a funeral of a young maiden. He tells of a garland of white paper flowers hung in the churchyard over her grave. In the mid-1700s, commonly white roses were draped around the pews of those young virgins of the parish who had died.

Flowers still play a great part in the showing of affection, as well as being used as an expression of sorrow, and we will take a look at the traditional meaning of various flowers in Chapter 4, as well as the connotations put on them by the Victorians.

Looking at religion

As we have already seen, there has always been a great deal of flower usage in religious ceremonies, both in the past and the present. Often, statues to gods were surrounded by flower offerings, and we can still see Egyptian records of the sun god, Ra, to this effect. The statues to Ra were actually crowned with woven flowers, in much the same way as statues of Christ often depict him wearing the woven crown of thorns associated with his death. Egyptian virgins assigned to work in the temples were often given crowns of helichrysum (also known as everlastings), serving as a symbol both of the everlasting power of the gods concerned and the everlasting service of the people. Flowers were used to decorate altars, and were used in the procession of the

annual Egyptian Festival of Shrines. Similar themes still exist today. In much the same way as, in our modern times, people buy wreaths of flowers to show respect at a funeral, in ancient times wreaths and flower offerings were left to die and fade. It is recorded that the Temple of Juno at Argos was burnt to the ground by a priestess who inadvertently set fire to the offerings when she fell asleep.

We have already seen that the Hebrews largely linked flower garlands to pagan practices, but in the Book of Judith, not forming part of the accepted Bible, we are told in the third chapter how Halofernes, chief captain of the Assyrian army, was received by Judith crowned with lilies in an attempt to protect herself from witchcraft, when he called for peace talks. Obviously finding this protection served its purpose, Judith was crowned with a wreath of olive branches when Holofernes was later put to death, the olive branch, as is still the case today, serving as a symbol of peace.

It is not unusual for pagan practices and Wiccan religious ceremonies to use flowers, as we have discussed, and records still exist of those people found guilty of practising pagan religions being bedecked with flowers at their execution.

In the Zoroastrian religion, emphasis is placed on flowers in their mid-autumn festival, known as Ayathrem Gahambar, in honour of plants, and represented in celebrations by flowers and fruits. This festival lasts for five days, and is one of the six annual festivals celebrated by the Zoroastrians. The other festivals seek to honour the creation of sky, water, earth, animals and human beings.

In Asia, the festival of Ching Ming sees the Chinese tidying graves and making offerings of food and drink but also of flowers. Indeed children sometimes wear sprigs of Pussy Willow on this day to avoid being born as dogs in the next life. Likewise, the birthday of Tam Kung is celebrated with parades of dancing dragons and offerings of flowers.

Within Hinduism, the festival of Makara Sankranti, which takes place when the sun enters Capricorn, sees people bathe in any holy river and exchange gifts and flowers. This is said to be a time to forget quarrels. At their festival of Shirvaratri, a day of worship dedicated to Lord Shiva, mango blossoms are offered, and many other festivals use flowers in a lesser way.

In Christendom, in addition to the placing of flowers and such offerings at Harvest Festival, and the decoration of churches with palms at Easter time, we also see the custom of placing advent wreaths in churches, as well as the lighting of candles. Buddhists use flowers to decorate their shrines at home, Jains Worship at their temples, known as Derasar, offering flowers and incense, and many other religions also actively use flowers, both at home and in their devotional activities.

FOLKLORE, FLOWERS AND PLANTS

There are many superstitions concerning flowers and plants, which we will discuss later, but most countries have their folklore, their traditions and their ceremonies stretching back in time, and a large proportion of these connect to flowers, plants and shrubs, marking seasonal changes. Many of these traditions are linked to specific times of the year, although the fern, which was said to drive away misfortune, could be picked at any time, its seeds then being collected in a white handkerchief and saved in a small white envelope, and permanently carried about.

May Day

May Day celebrations are commonplace, and often link to gods or goddesses. One tradition in Italy was the festival to the goddess Flora, which took place either in late April or early May. Presided over by a young woman bedecked in a garland of flowers, this was a perennial reminder that the colour and richness of nature was indeed a gift from the gods. Although less common than in years gone by, the use of the maypole and the bedecking of the May Queen still features as part of the celebrations to welcome summer. At one time, most English villages had their own maypole, and many schools also had a maypole, around which children would

dance and weave the ribbons. The maypole would originally have been cut from a tree-trunk, with its branches removed, and decorated with flowers and ribbons. It was traditional for virgins to dance around the pole, hopeful of meeting a suitable mate – again, the link with fertility. It was also traditional for a young maiden, seeking a partner, to plant a yarrow in her front garden, in order to attract a future mate. Similarly, rosemary, if gathered on Midsummer's Day, or a red rose, were considered to have much the same power in attracting a future partner, especially so if the rose was picked with the dew still on it and placed in a silver vase. Likewise it is worthwhile noting that the Oak King, incorporated in the pagan festivals of Beltane and Lughnasadh along with the Holly King, was said to die on the eve of May Day, consummating his love, to be reborn again so that the earth may be renewed.

Trees and plants have long played an integral part in the May pageant. In Cornwall for example, there is a custom which uses the young branches of a sycamore tree for making into whistles, the idea being that these whistles could be used to drive out evil spirits. Many people will also have heard of the Cornish Helston Furry, where locals dance through the streets, their hats and clothing decorated with flowers. Originally, this was a May-time celebration, based on fertility rites and ensuring a successful harvest in the months to come. Both men and women would gather around bonfires, bedecked in flowers, and dance the night away, the ashes of the bonfire then being sprinkled on the fields in order to ensure a good crop.

Midsummer Day

The picking of marigolds or marshmallow flowers at dusk on Midsummer Day was thought to help patch up quarrels with loved ones. If gathered in silence and placed in a jug of water on an outside windowsill, it was said that the quarrel would be resolved within three weeks, and that someone who had left home would return. Traditionally, it was also felt that picking a bunch of violets or a spray of hops on Midsummer Day would help to increase the

wealth of the person concerned. In the Middle Ages, women worried that their husband or lover was straying, dug up earth from around his footprints, sowed marigold seeds in it, and hoped that this would bring him back to the straight and narrow. Around the same time, cyclamen and fern seeds put into cakes were recommended as being good for amorous intentions, but the seeds had to be gathered on Midsummer's Eve by a maiden, and in the correct way only! A Bible had to be placed under the plant, and the seeds shaken into a pewter dish with a hazelwood fork. The plant was not to be touched by human hand, as torment by demons would result!

Well dressing is a tradition which continues in many Derbyshire towns, especially in Buxton, where on the nearest Thursday to Midsummer, flowers decorate the town.

Another ancient Midsummer festival at which flowers and plants were used was the festival to St John, which falls on 24 June. During St John's Eve, bonfires were lit and various plants sacrificed to St John – St John's wort, fennel, bracken, orpine, plantain, daisy, mugwort, yarrow, ivy and corn marigold. These were passed through the smoke from the fire in order to cleanse them and strengthen their powers, and then often hung up in domestic or agricultural settings to protect against witchcraft and lightning.

Christmas

The pagan Holly King rules from midsummer to midwinter, which is why the use of holly is popular at Christmas. The holly bush was linked by various peoples with the wren, and the wintertime ceremony Hunting the Wren can be traced back as far as ancient Greece and Rome, where it links with both the holly and ivy plants. Various traditions using holly still exist in certain places – Ireland, for example, still sees groups of adult musicians, singers and dancers, known as 'wren boys' travelling from house to house in County Clare, wearing conical straw hats and carrying a wren statue on a holly branch.

Holly was regarded by ancient peoples as a masculine plant, possibly due to its prickly leaves, while the ivy was thought to be a

feminine plant. As such, the intertwining of the two to make wreaths and garlands symbolised the linking of the male and female principles, the prospect of renewal and regrowth, of fertility and rebirth. Holly was, incidentally, once thought to be a cure for worms.

The use of holly, ivy and mistletoe at Christmas time goes way back in history. The Romans considered holly to be a symbol of goodwill and friendliness, as also was the laurel. During the period of Saturnalia, which corresponds roughly to the Christian festival of Christmas, the Romans sent holly branches to all their friends as a token of goodwill and benevolence, and put out laurel wreaths on their doorways, as a sign of a friendly greeting to passers-by. The word 'holly' itself is said to be derived from the word 'holy', thus its usage in festivals to gods is explained.

It was thought that holly could protect a household, so large bunches of holly were traditionally hung over doorways at the end of the year, and the bush was often planted near houses to protect against harm from thunder and lightning. In certain rural areas, it was felt that a bunch of holly placed near a cowshed or stable on Christmas Eve would protect the animals. Many people still take a piece of holly from church decorations at Christmas, as a protection against harm during the coming year. In Northern Europe, it was thought that the wood spirits would find shelter in the bunches of holly hung above the doors, and consequently good luck would come to the householder who has been charitable enough to provide shelter for the spirits.

Said to guard its wearer against witchcraft (witches traditionally being scared of the plant, possibly because of its connection with anything holy), the holly plant was also commonly fastened to the beds of virgin girls at Christmas time, to guard against evil during the coming year, and was given to single girls at New Year festivals as a guarantee of finding a partner. It was also said that placing nine holly leaves within a nine-knotted handkerchief would ensure the maiden would dream of her future mate.

With the spread of Christianity, holly was taken as symbolic of the crown of thorns worn by Jesus, and the red berries of the plant were a reminder of the blood which Jesus shed on behalf of mankind.

Various legends and myths sprang up around this central theme of holly and Christ, one of which is that a holly bush appeared on the ground immediately after Jesus was resurrected, and another being that the cross was made of holly wood, with the berries originally having been yellow and changing to red when the blood of Jesus fell on them. The Christmas carol 'The Holly and the Ivy' makes reference to the holly being 'the crown'.

Mistletoe was a sacred plant to the Druids, and it is thought that the tradition of kissing under a spring of mistletoe began as part of a Druidic ritual. The kiss was felt to be a symbol of human fertility, and it was believed that kissing under the mistletoe would bring back to life plants which were at that time dormant. Legend states that for every kiss beneath the mistletoe, a berry should be removed, and the kissing should stop only when all the berries have disappeared. At the time of the winter solstice, according to the Roman Pliny, the Druids would seek out a tree on which mistletoe grew. They considered that if the plant was found growing on an oak tree, this was most favourable, the oak being a sacred tree in its own right. Mistletoe can, however, also be found on apple and pear trees. The mistletoe was then cut, using a sacred golden knife or sickle, and would fall on to a white cloth (it should never touch the ground) laid at the base of the tree, and then a sacrifice took place at the foot of the tree. The sprays of mistletoe were then blessed by the Chief Druid, who laid it beneath the altar stone for three days, after which it was handed out to those assembled around, to protect them from evil during the coming 12 months. As it was connected to protection, it was also considered powerful against the effects of witchcraft, and placing mistletoe beneath one's pillow was said to ensure a nightmare-free sleep.

Thought by many ancient peoples to be a cure for anything, mistletoe became known as the golden bough and features in many superstitions worldwide, more of which in Chapter 3. Mistletoe was commonly hung over doorways as a symbol of peace and hospitality, in much the same way as holly, the two being closely linked. As the mistletoe was seen to survive in the harshest of

conditions, it was also considered to be a symbol of immortality, and again its links with Christianity, and with Jesus Christ in particular, cannot be ignored.

The ancient peoples also used mistletoe in health care, and native North Americans have long used mistletoe tea as a remedy for measles, toothache and dog bites. Others use it to treat chilblains, and more recently, at the end of the nineteenth century, mistletoe was used as an infusion, a wine or a powder, and mixed with honey was a treatment for whooping cough. The berries and leaves were boiled in water or milk, and the resultant mixture was used to help alleviate the pain of gout and rheumatism.

Ivy, another evergreen, and a plant which often entwines itself around other plants and trees, is often connected to everlasting life, although conversely it could be viewed as being something weak in nature, having to cling to other more hardy and sturdy plants in order to survive. Its links to everlasting life, and its connections with mistletoe and holly, also connect it to the Christmas period. Ivy was used, in past times, for divination purposes; a healthy leaf was left in a basin of water from New Years Eve until after twelfth night, when it was used for foretelling the future. If the leaf was still fresh and green, it was assumed that the year ahead would be good, whereas if the leaf was black, illness was indicated. At one time, wearing a garland of ivy around the head was said to prevent hair loss, and many medical preparations were also made from the ivy leaf. Juices from its leaves if mixed with hot water and inhaled were said to help relieve the symptoms of colds, while when mixed with a cream or lotion, ivy was said to help cure skin complaints.

Rosemary was once popular at the end of the year in decorations, and as it was thought to help with the memory and keep people young, a custom of crushing fresh rosemary and baking it in biscuits at the festive season developed. **Honesty**, a plant with lovely silvery pods, was also once used in flower arrangements at Christmas, and was said to be lucky bringing wealth during the coming year, the silver pods resembling money and coinage.

Rosemary

FLOWERS AND PLANTS IN SHAKESPEARE'S PLAYS

Those interested in Shakespeare might already know that many flowers were named in his plays. The gillyflower features in *The Winter's Tale*, the cowslip in *A Midsummer Night's Dream* and pansies in *Hamlet*. Another plant mentioned in *Hamlet* as being 'for remembrance' is rosemary. Used widely by the Greeks for both cooking and at shrines where it was burnt, it was also a sacred plant to the Romans, and was used throughout the Middle Ages in exorcisms, and in sickrooms as a means of reducing disease. Rosemary has strong antiseptic properties, can delay putrefaction in meat, can hide any underlying bad tastes, and is also a brain stimulant. It is known to help with respiratory problems.

Another plant used prominently in Shakespeare's times was deadly nightshade (belladonna). Witches throughout medieval Europe used the plant in their spells and ointments. The whole plant is poisonous, due to the presence of alkaloids such as hyoscyamine. Deadly nightshade was mentioned by Shakespeare in *Macbeth*, where it was used to knock out the invading Danes. Eye drops were and still are sometimes made from belladonna, and it is used to great effect in many homoeopathic preparations.

2 Looking at colour

Most of us take the ability to see for granted. People who have studied the effect that colour has on our lives suggest that colour does more to our inner selves than just 'register'. It affects us at a subconscious level. In this chapter, we will look at colour, and see how bringing colour into our homes in the form of flowers can help to lift our spirits and ease our state of mind. We will also look at which colours are said to help us in specific areas, and how we can make use of colour in flower decorations.

Changing the colours around us

Colour is wonderful – we should appreciate it. It gives an added 'dimension' to the different objects we see around us. Let's pretend for a moment that colour doesn't exist, and that everything appears in various shades of grey. Knowing how we might feel on a day when there is no sunshine – common in the United Kingdom especially in wintertime – we can understand how seeing everything in shades of grey must take away a lot of pleasure from our inner selves.

We can see both the colour of an object, and also colour patterns – how some gardens are planted with colours all aimed to blend together, or how the colours of some plants and flowers make them really stand out to make a feature of the area in which they are sited. On a visit to the Netherlands many years ago, I noticed how

the landscape can be totally transformed by acres of tulips, in their many shades of reds and yellows. Harvest time with its pale yellows, interspersed with the red of poppies is another wonderful sight to behold, and mountainous or moorland areas where there are acres of yellow gorse, russet bramble and mauve heather are further examples. I am sure that you can point to various times of year and favourite places when the colour of the flowers, trees and shrubs make an impact on your senses.

Not only is the planet Earth itself and all that is on it a beautiful and colourful sight, but so is the sky. It is wonderful to see the colours of the sky change; the warm reds, oranges, pinks and yellows especially create a stunning scene. You might also see green in the sky – what is known as the 'green flash', if the conditions are right, at the last moment of a sunset. Even rarer is the blue flash. As we will learn later, blue light waves have a shorter wavelength than red and yellow, and this is one of the reasons why the sky appears blue when the sun is well above the horizon on a clear day.

During the course of a year there are many festivals where flowers play a part in brightening up the proceedings. One such springtime ritual is the Battle of Flowers in Jersey in the Channel Islands and also at Cannes, and the five flower festivals of the Orient.

We also use flowers in our homes, sometimes in elaborate decorations, or just in simple arrangements. Some really striking flower arrangements can be made using vibrant colours such as red and yellow, and, at times of dreary weather, making such a prominent display of flowers can give a cheerful aspect to a room and also help to cheer up the people within it. More about flower arrangements later though! Within the world of nature, we have the exotic colours of species of flowers and trees, changing with the seasons, as the flowers and buds burst forth.

We certainly are fortunate to be able to see colour. It is said that beauty is in the eye of the beholder, and it is fair to say that many people just do not take the time to *see* the beauty of the colours which surround them. Colour, however, can also affect our moods, whether we acknowledge the colour or not. Most people will acknowledge that they often feel better in clothes of one colour than

another. People might compliment us on how a certain colour suits us, but we may not feel right wearing it, and so consequently never wear the outfit again. Likewise, we often change our choices in colour of clothing, and these changing colour preferences can tell us a lot about our physical and mental states.

There are many sayings in the English language concerning colour. A few examples include: 'I saw red' meaning 'I was angry'; 'I felt blue', meaning 'I felt depressed'; 'I am feeling in the pink today', meaning 'I feel good about myself today'. Another phrase is 'such and such an event coloured my thinking'. There are, no doubt, many more expressions known to you. People talk about being 'in a black mood' meaning that they are either depressed or just miserable. In nature, there are fortunately few naturally black flowers or plants. The tradition of wearing black at times of death, or mourning, started in all probability during Victorian times; it is known that following Prince Albert's death, Queen Victoria always wore black. Interestingly, some people, the Chinese and Muslims for example, consider white to be the colour of death, because, especially to the Chinese, it represents happiness and prosperity in the next world.

BRINGING COLOUR INTO OUR homes

Following on from work carried out at the beginning of the twentieth century by Rudolf Steiner, it has become accepted that colour can alter people's mental and physical states; hospitals especially, as well as prisons, offices and shops, seek to use colours which will bring about the best response from people. Some employers will go as far as engaging psychologists to carry out a detailed assessment of job applicants by testing their colour preferences. It has also been established under test conditions that, even if a person is blindfolded or indeed blind, colour can affect his or her physical well-being.

Work carried out by Marie Louise Lacy, of the International Association for Colour Therapy, has given us further insights into the

use of colour. Similarly, scientific tests on the colour of food have established a definite link between foods of a certain colour and health benefits. For this reason, the Bristol Cancer Centre actively uses its knowledge of colour and health in the treatment and diet of cancer patients.

Linking a knowledge of colour and herbalism has lead to the development of a form of therapy known as Aura Soma, using coloured oils with various fragrances, which can act as mere decoration when placed in their bottles in the correct light, or which can be used to work on the chakra systems of the body – the energy centres generally accepted to follow the line of the spine, or on other areas where imbalance is present. Aura Soma was developed by Vicky Wall, who had for some time been making herbal preparations. Two balanced herb oils are placed within one bottle, which when shaken will blend and then separate. These balance oils are designed to help restore health when used in combination with herbs and essential oils, through the power of colour, and are recommended for use on any part of the body, especially for night application. Aura Soma uses 49 preparations, which have been developed from an original five, some single colours and a few dual-colour combinations. I have used Aura Soma, and have, within my collection of various types of herbal and aromatherapy treatments, a bottle of pink over purple Aura Soma displayed in the correct lighting, which I sometimes use on my skin. Linked to the chakra system, more of which later, the original five colours of Aura Soma are yellow over red (called sunset), yellow (sunlight), green over blue (heart), blue (peace) and violet over blue (Rescue Remedy).

In many parts of the world, at the Christmas period, families have a Christmas tree, which they decorate with coloured baubles, lights and candles. This is another way of bringing colour into the home to brighten up the surroundings, help to lift spirits, and especially in Europe relieve the darkness during the daytime, the result of the reduction in sunshine, light and warmth. It is now established that seasonal deficiency illness (known as SAD) really does exist, and brings about depression, feelings of sadness, and so on, because of the lack of natural light and colour in our world at wintertime. It is thought by many that freesias, which have bright colours and a

lovely smell, can help in the healing of mind and emotions, and so those suffering from SAD might do well to try introducing freesias into their homes. Likewise, the colour pink, considered by many to be the colour of unconditional love and to help in problems with communication, could suggest the giving of pink roses, which will soothe, warm and relax, while yellow flowers, especially roses (again) or daffodils, will help to brighten up the spirits of someone who is getting over an illness.

COLOUR ENERGIES

It is generally accepted that energies are given off by different colours. These energies are known as colour rays. In order to benefit from these rays, we need to know a little about each colour, how it can help us and how it can work against us. Armed with this information, we can then take a look at which flowers should be introduced to both the house and the garden, in order to achieve what we want. We can also think of incorporating these colours into our home decorations or furnishings, or using various colours of lightbulb to create the right effect. We should, however, where possible try to balance stronger colours by their opposite number, for example red and green, in order to create a soothing environment. Incidentally colour healing, also known as chromotherapy, is also something we may wish to consider using. It is also worth noting that using colour and water, known as hydrochromopathy, used both for effect and as a medicine, has been popular in India for many centuries.

In this book we will concentrate on the seven rainbow or prismatic colours – red, orange, yellow, green, blue, indigo and violet, and briefly link them to the chakra centres in the body, shown in the illustration on page 26. *Chakras for beginners*, another book in this series, will help those who wish to learn more about body energies. Each chakra is like a lotus, the roots being hidden in the deep, dark mud, with an ever-increasing desire by the plant to push upwards, through the waters, to reach the light at the surface and then to bloom. All chakras can be opened, like the petals of a flower, and information is given on specific flowers which you might wish to try in relation to each chakra, if undergoing meditation especially. I

would stress that the flowers indicated are guidelines only. You may wish to experiment with other flowers within the colouring groups. In addition, colours also relate to days of the week, and it is thought by some that use of the colour for that particular day will enhance well-being. Likewise, in nearly all cases, herbs, incenses and perfumes are also assigned to a day and a colour, and this information will also be given here.

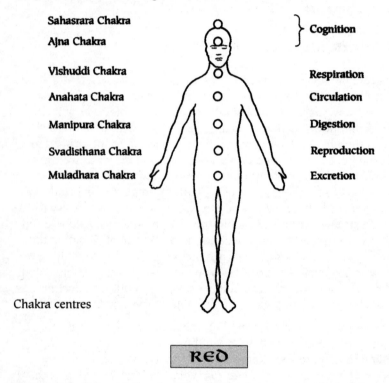

Sahasrara Chakra
Ajna Chakra
} Cognition

Vishuddi Chakra — Respiration
Anahata Chakra — Circulation
Manipura Chakra — Digestion
Svadisthana Chakra — Reproduction
Muladhara Chakra — Excretion

Chakra centres

RED

This has the longest wavelength and the fastest rate of vibration.

Day Tuesday
Herb Urtica
Perfume Civet
Incense Lig. Aloes.
Musical note Doh

Chakra centre and basic meaning   Linked with the base or root chakra situated at the base of the spine, red connects with energy. Connected with Mars, it stands for aggression, passion, life and lust. Also connected to Apollo, it concerns energy, strength, courage and valour. People still use the expression 'red letter day' as in earlier times, the saints' days were written in red in the calendar, as a symbol of the blood of the martyrs.

Red and white together, as we have seen, link with illness and death, whilst red and black are said to link to Satan. In alchemy, the Red King is well known.

Red in the sky   In the evening, there are red rays in the sky, and a beautiful sunset in itself can help to lift our spirits.

Red in our surroundings   Red is a warm, invigorating colour which can stimulate us and lift us, but to the ancient Celts was a foreteller of disaster, probably because of its resemblance to blood. Wearing red can help us to feel more dynamic, but can also affect our blood pressure and production of red blood cells, a fact borne out by scientific tests using red lights. Some reds can be just a little too much, and too much exposure to red can irritate inflammatory conditions such as arthritis. Red is the colour of passion, as well as anger, so we should look for softer shades of red if we merely need a little lift. If we are already tense, the red ray will only bring about more tension or anger. Being the colour of blood, and therefore seen as the colour of life, red is symbolic of health, strength, courage and physical love; gypsies used to wear red at funerals to symbolise physical life and energy.

Red flowers to consider   The base chakra is said to have only four petals, and consequently any flowers associated with this should, preferably, have four petals, although this is not a hard-and-fast rule. You might wish to try using poppies, their bright red colour being particularly suited to this chakra, or alternatively try roses, even though they have considerably more petals. Other red flowers you might wish to try include snapdragon, some dahlias, sweet bergamot, or geranium.

ORANGE

This is the colour of the sun, and of light, heat and vitality.

Day Sunday
Herb Juniper
Perfume Neroli (made from the orange blossom)
Incense Mastic
Musical note Re

Chakra centre and basic meaning Connected to the sacral chakra located close to the reproductive organs, the colour orange activates the spleen, kidneys and adrenal glands. Used in colour therapy fields for healing of the respiratory system, it is a stimulant and reduces tiredness and depression. Said to be the colour of prana, ch'i or the life force, it concerns health and well-being. If this chakra centre is blocked, the person concerned can be over-ambitious, even domineering.

Orange in the sky Orange is seen often in the sky in the early afternoon. It is thought that during this time, using the orange ray, we can find true self-expression, be at our most creative and happy.

Orange in our surroundings Relieving us of depression, fears and inhibitions, the colour will help to lift us gently and gradually. Although orange is used by therapists in work with autistic children, too much exposure to the colour can lead to selfish ambition and pride taking control. Orange is said to be the colour which will aid relationships, helping to soothe difficulties. Those who are having a bad patch are advised to consider introducing some orange into their homes, irrespective of the chakra centre to which it relates.

Orange flowers to consider Students of chakras, will know the petals of the chakra to be vermilion even though the colour orange will connect here. However, you can think in terms of the carthamnus tinctoris, a lovely orange colour, or more conventionally some chrysanthemums or marigolds. Other orange flowers to consider might include the montbretia, wallflower, dahlia and some varieties of primrose.

yellow

Stimulating, bright and cheerful, this is the colour of wisdom.

Day Wednesday
Herb Coriander
Perfume Lavender
Incense Cinnamon
Musical note Mi

Chakra centre and basic meaning Yellow connects to the solar plexus chakra and is concerned with clarity. It is a colour often used by therapists to treat menstrual problems, and it is also used for problems with the pancreas, liver and spleen. It helps with confidence, enhances concentration and well-being, and increases creativity and optimism. It also links with communication, and it is interesting that Wednesday, as a day, links with Mercury, the god of communication. Yellow is often thought to link to cowardice and deceipt, but being the colour of the sun, it is also symbolic of reason and logical thought, not interrupted by emotion. Too much yellow can cause problems with lack of action, apathy and general indecisiveness. Linked to the robes of the Buddhist monks, it is symbolic to many of humility, meekness and renunciation.

Yellow in the sky Prominent in the morning skies, just as the light rises, this colour gives hope for a bright day.

Yellow in our surroundings Yellow will help with logical thought production, and is thought to help with skin ailments and weight fluctuation. Too much exposure to yellow will give rise to feelings of insecurity and loss of direction.

Yellow flowers to consider The colour yellow is cheery, resemblant of the warmth of summer. Considered by many to be the floral representative of the solar wheel, the sunflower is said to symbolise adoration and perfection. It is, incidentally, the symbol of Christian obedience to many, since all day it faces the 'sun' of Christ. Roses can also be a good flower to consider, as can yellow tulips or yellow lilies. Within the world of wild flowers, we also have

the buttercup, while other flowers you may wish to consider could include fennel, golden-bell, mahonia, honeysuckle, winter-flowering jasmine or the golden rod.

GREEN

The colour of nature, and a great healer and promoter of restfulness.

Day   Friday
Herb   Verbena
Perfume   Stephanotis
Incense   Saffron
Musical note   Fah

Chakra centre and basic meaning   This colour connects to the heart chakra. Green is a colour associated with healing, so it is for this reason that many hospitals use green in their wards, and as most plants and flowers will have at least some green in their leaves and overall colour, it is not surprising that so many people bring plants and flowers into hospitals as gifts for patients, along with, perhaps, green grapes! Linked to Venus, and also with the world of elves, sprites and fairies, many people consider it a folly to wear green, because to do so would upset the fairy folk. Combining blue which connects with the heavens and yellow which connects with the earth, it can cause problems if used or worn in excess, by leading to sensationalism.

Green in the sky   Visible in the sky just before sunrise, green gives us hope for the future, promotes balanced judgement and concerns growth of potential for success in the future.

Green in our surroundings   Calming, as well as acting as a tonic and revitaliser, green can help with balancing the thymus gland, in the treatment of headaches, colds and heart problems. It is also useful in treating shock, being a calmative, and can help reduce blood pressure and speed up the body's natural healing processes. Green is the colour of many bank notes, therefore green is associated with financial concerns and success. It is also said to be the colour of envy.

Green flowers to consider   Although there are few green flowers, there are always various greens around in the world of nature that

can be used with the heart chakra. Evergreens such as ivy or holly are a good idea, as are any leaves or bushes, and herbs especially are worthwhile considering. However, as most people will have their own preferences for flowers that they link to affairs of the heart (including, obviously, roses), you may wish to use a flower of your choice when working with this chakra.

BLUE

A spiritual colour and good all-round healer.

Day Thursday
Herb Cedar
Perfume Ambergris
Incense Nutmeg
Musical note Soh

Chakra centre and basic meaning Blue is associated with the throat chakra, and concerns communication. The colour of lapis lazuli, a gemstone very popular at the time of the ancient Egyptians and used extensively in tomb decorations, blue will help calm the nerves, correct imbalances in the thyroid gland and reduce blood pressure, being a natural tranquilliser. Associated with Jupiter and all the sky gods, it is said to be the colour of dreams, of the unconscious mind, and thus of the psychic or sensitive. Connected in Christendom to Mary, it is also symbolic of the mother figure.

Blue in the sky Blue is visible in the early morning sky, other than on warm, summer days when the whole sky appears to be blue. It can help to lift our spirits, give us faith for a better day, and trust for the future.

Blue in our surroundings Water, closely associated with the colour blue, will help to encourage peacefulness and tranquillity, and this is possibly one of the many reason why holidays by the seaside are popular. Blue is also useful in the treatment of rheumatism, fevers, burns and inflammations.

Blue flowers to consider A lovely blue to use with this chakra centre is that of the cornflower. Various stocks also have amongst them an attractive blue, and other flowers to consider could include

the brodiaea, cupid's dart, hyacinth, lupin, forget-me-not, or periwinkle. Blue hyacinths are thought to help cleanse and purify an atmosphere.

INDIGO

Indigo is also known as midnight blue and is the most powerful colour ray. Indigo does not have any links with day, herb, perfume or incense.

Musical note   Lah

Chakra centre and basic meaning   Associated with the unfolding of spirituality, indigo is the colour of infinity and intuition and is linked to the chakra which the ancient Egyptians termed the 'third eye'. Connected with Saturn, Kali, Isis and darkness, it is symbolic of death and the passing of time.

Indigo in the sky   Indigo is visible in our skies around midnight, and makes for a beautiful tranquil feeling.

Indigo in our surroundings   Most writers will acknowledge that indigo can help to clear writing blocks, and is also a useful colour in meditation. Used by colour therapists for healing of emotional disorders, it is indeed a powerful colour, promoting wisdom and higher spirituality.

Indigo flowers to consider   Few flowers adequately match the indigo colour, and you must use your judgement when dealing with this chakra area, although borage does come close.

VIOLET

Associated with royalty, with mysticism and with religion. Violet does not have any links with day, herb, perfume or incense.

Musical note   Ti

Chakra centre and basic meaning   This colour is associated with the crown chakra, balances the pituitary gland, and helps with nervousness, especially in women. Connected with devotion, religion and spirituality, this colour is the colour of the Moon and

LIFELING AT COLOUR

the White Queen in alchemy. Associated also with Mary Magdalene, it is connected to sorrow and repentance.

Violet in the sky Said to be the ray of sacrifice and purification, violet is visible in the sky in the late evening, a time when meditation can be particularly beneficial. Meditation itself will help to cleanse the mind, and it is not therefore surprising to discover that many famous people, Wagner and Leonardo da Vinci being just two, actively used violet in their surroundings and for meditation.

Violet in our surroundings Do be careful here, as too much purple or violet, especially in clothing, can help make those who are already a little sad even more depressed.

Violet flowers to consider What better than the violet itself. Others you could consider might include the Peruvian lily, which can be found in various colours including a lovely purple hue, the michaelmas daisy, wallflower, sword lily, lilac or lavender.

White and black

Although not recognised as existent by many, an eighth chakra is believed by some to be located above the head and which controls all the other chakras. Said to lie within the aura of the person, this chakra relates to **white**, and those wishing to meditate or reactivate

Lily-of-the-valley

all their chakra centres, or who wish to think in terms of overall healing, both physical and emotional, might wish to use white flowers for this purpose. I think white lilies are the best flowers here, but others would suggest white roses, lily-of-the-valley, snowdrops, Christmas rose, or common white jasmine. White also links with Monday, with the poppy, with nicotiana as a perfume and with myrtle as an incense.

Likewise **black**, thought by many to link with death, relates to Saturday, to the herb hellebore, to the violet perfume and to the peppermint incense.

ChildReN aNd colour

Children, as well as adults, will benefit from the use of colours, and as some children can be oversensitive to smells and are certainly more likely than adults to knock over flowers and plants, you may wish to consider introducing colour in another way. Children are generally interested in colour. Most will immediately tell you their favourite colour, know what they like and what they don't and react accordingly. As children move towards adolescence, their interest in colour can alter dramatically, and it is normally around this time that teenagers start to want to choose and decorate their own bedrooms, often in colours considered bizarre by their parents. Many children go through a stage of being interested in black and dark colours. Normally it is a passing phase, so parents shouldn't be overly concerned, unless they notice other worrying features in the behaviour of their children.

Babies normally react if placed in pastel shades; most mothers automatically sense this, finding out to their cost that placing a baby in a powerful colour, like bright yellow, can produce tantrums, overexcitement and other problems. Babies also respond better in a light, warm environment, and again the use of lighter colours in furnishings, plants, flowers and decoration is worth considering. If you feel that the colour of lighting has no impact, especially on children, try introducing a pink light in a child's bedroom and watch the sleep pattern improve.

CHANGING TASTE IN FLOWERS AND COLOURS

Over the years flower usage and colour preferences have changed, and it is quite interesting to take a brief look at how different generations have used flowers and colours in the home. We'll start with the Victorians, who adored flowers so much that they devised languages for them (more of which in Chapter 4).

Flowers were everywhere in the Victorian home. Not only were flowers in the home, but they also featured in poetry (Wordsworth's 'Daffodils'), inspired paintings and textile design, and decorated hats and dresses. The Victorians were neat and precise in their use of flowers. Their gardens were usually laid out in ordered fashion, greenhouses became popular, with rose nurseries springing up in many areas. Roses were very popular with the Victorians, and table decorations, especially, were highly elaborate with tiers of flowers, lots of foliage and hothouse flowers where possible to create impact. Popular colours at the time were bright reds and yellows.

With the arrival of the Edwardian era, a more rigid type of formality came into play, and roses still featured in most homes. People whose income was lower bought flowers from street sellers who sold little posies of violets or other sweet-smelling flowers. Set patterns and forms were commonplace in arrangements.

Following the end of the First World War, and the progression into a more jovial era, a more relaxed use of flowers became the norm, with both wild and garden flowers being seen together in arrangements, as had been the case in medieval times. Colour combinations were less formal, and mauve was particularly popular.

Following the Second World War, a period of rationing and shortages saw little use of flowers other than for special occasions, or as a buttonhole. The 1950s, however, saw an explosion of colour, with the idea being the bigger and brasher the better. People became influenced by the films they saw at the cinema, and anything daring, bright and undesigned was popular. Flowers like the gladioli and iris

Delphinium

were favourites, and, although flower shops had a hard time, many local gardeners found themselves growing flowers and plants never before tried.

In 1960s design there was a predominance of black and white and also of what were called 'op-art' colourings. In fact, it was a time when anything was acceptable, and also the decade when the British were first introduced to the concept of the 'garden centres'. In the 1960s and 1970s, any colour was in vogue, and not only was it popular to use any colour, but almost any colours were mixed together in flower arrangements. Likewise, especially around the time of the influx of Scandinavian furniture and influences, more clean-cut designs in home decorations, furniture and fewer decorations came into vogue. Furniture designs used black and chrome, and glass-topped dining tables, often in smoked glass, were all the rage. Glass vases also underwent a revival, and most flower decorations, seemingly just thrown together, were placed on coffee tables in glass vases.

As we head into the new millennium, more colour co-ordinated flower decorations appear to be popular, although the rose is still as popular as it ever was, especially to lovers of romance.

USING FLOWERS IN DECORATIONS

I am by no means an expert when it comes to making flower decorations. However, I have friends who are, and what follows are some tips recommended by them on creating favourable colour combinations in flower decorations and arrangements around the home. If you are a novice, I would suggest that you allow yourself ample time for all the necessary work, so that it isn't rushed, and you don't get yourself tense by, for example, leaving yourself ten minutes before a dinner party to get it organised. After all, you wouldn't want your flower decoration to fall apart during the evening because you haven't spent an adequate amount of time assembling it. Flower arranging can be therapeutic, and some of the best arrangements are the simplest! We will now concentrate on getting colour into our homes, and how to make the most of the flowers and colours we have at our disposal.

LOCATION, DESIGN AND BALANCE

If you have a fireplace, and wish to fill the space with something when it is not in use, what better than a simple decoration of flowers? This is just one example of the ideas you can use to transform your home using flowers. Of course, flowers are not limited to particular seasons. Any time of the year we can add colour to our homes and to our lives by bringing in some flowers.

Choosing seasonal shades can greatly enhance a room, imitating the colours of nature, not only of flowers but also of fruits and shrubs. Spring colours can be pale lilacs and pinks, but also the colour of apple blossom or a combination of pale yellows and white. Summer colours include strawberry, apricot and other fruit colours, while autumn shades, russets, golds and reds, can also add something to a room. Likewise at the end of the year, when it may be cold outside and there may not be much colour in the gardens, try using some

bright colours indoors, such as striking red poinsettias or Christmas roses with their pure white flowers, as well as other flowers now available throughout the year, thanks to imports from other countries. Remember also to look at wild flowers (check first, that the flowers you wish to pick are not a protected species), at common thistles and gorses, and, especially at the end of the year when bought flowers are expensive, add extra colour with some fruit.

One thing to remember when using flowers to decorate a room is that clusters of any colour, even pale colours, can be as dominant in a design as the most carefully chosen deep-coloured flowers. It is the size and the placement within the decoration which count.

Location

A striking way of using a flower decoration to maximum effect is to place flowers in front of a mirror or any object which will reflect both the light and the colour of the flowers. If you have such a place, do make the most of it. Some people also have alcoves strategically lit for flower decorations. Before you start, however, do make sure that you look at the colours already in the room, and consider actually arranging the flowers in the intended location, rather than making the decoration in the kitchen then taking them into the room and finding it just doesn't work.

Don't be afraid to experiment a little. If you are putting your display on an oak table, or on something darker, think how that will react with the colours you have chosen. Look at the lighting in the room, and perhaps place your decoration in a spot where the natural lighting will help. You might also wish to consider having a hanging basket outside your door, or in the porch area if you have one, irrespective of the time of year.

If you wish to create a centrepiece for your dinner table, especially if you are hoping to attract a little romance into the proceedings, you might like to add candles. Their effect will enhance a special meal. Likewise, if you wish to invest in a few floating candles, float them in a bowl of water near to a special arrangement to add that little bit of extra 'glow'. Remember, however, that if you are using candles or

nightlights, keep them away from the flowers so that the whole thing doesn't go up in flames.

Choosing the Flowers

What do you wish to achieve? You should ask this at the outset. Are you looking for something which blends in, or are you looking for something which will make a statement? Having decided, you should then consider colours and investigate what flowers are available to you. There are many you could choose, but it is important that you like the flowers themselves, enjoy their fragrance, and then make sure that the flowers you decide upon are easily obtainable – look in your garden for guidance. Also decide whether you are going to buy flowers; think about the cost, especially if finances are limited. Decide how many flowers you might need, and what else you need for the decoration. Look at the space you have to fill.

Think of the shape of the design you want, the height and width: don't just think in terms of rounded shapes, with larger blooms and stalks on the outer edges of your arrangements and smaller blooms at the centre; think also of triangles, rectangles or even half-circles. Also think in terms of symmetry – make sure both sides balance. Remember to include some greenery, as it can act as a buffer between two strong colours. Roses and orchids make a nice combination – think about the shape and form of the flowers too, and create an overall pattern which harmonises. You also have to make sure that you don't choose flowers which are ill-matched in scale. For example, you wouldn't want to place gladioli next to a group of lilies-of-the-valley. It just wouldn't work. You need to think of flowers of similar sizes.

Remember what we have learnt about colour and how it affects us. If you want to create a striking arrangement, reds, yellows and oranges work, but remember what we have already learnt about these colours, and don't make the arrangements too startling. If you want something a little more soothing, think delicate flowers, in blue-pinks, mauves, blues and softer tones. Also think in terms of grey or silvery foliage, and consider the shape of the leaves in your foliage – using pointed foliage, such as the leaves of flax, can make

an interesting arrangement, and mixing in some dried ears of wheat will work well at any time of year. You might also wish to consider a blending of all one colour, from pale to dark, but also remember to make sure that the design is suitable, and think about having a focal point – what is sometimes called the 'heart' of the arrangement. This need not be a single flower – a group of four or five flowers of varying sizes might be more interesting, or you might consider three flowers surrounded by leaves.

Good summer colours are oranges, yellows and blues. White also works well in summertime. Pale colours work well at any time, and in winter a splash of red or green will help cheer up the cold evenings. Silver and gold also work well in wintertime, and dried flowers, with a few gold- or silver-painted cones and leaves, or seasonal clusters of berries or fruit, will help to make a beautiful arrangement.

If you still feel undecided, take a look at the fabrics you have in your room, or some of the ornaments. See what colours go with each other, and which ones you personally feel comfortable with, and try to find flowers which will match. You may, however, wish to have all the same flowers of the same colour. In this case, try not to use blooms of the same height, and think about introducing some other colours by varying the foliage to add interest.

Containers

You don't necessarily have to use a vase or container, although if you do, you should make sure that the colour complements your arrangement, and don't put large flowers into a container which is obviously too small to balance properly. Despite what we have said about vases, remember that a circular base or bowl really does demand a circular design, and also remember that the first placement of flowers must be firm, as the rest of the arrangement will be built around it. You may also wish to experiment with different containers. Think about using a copper tea-urn for example, a large wine glass or other more unusual containers. I have seen very effective arrangements in things as diverse as a vinegar jar and a warming pan.

Some flower decorations

There is now a wonderful material called florists' foam, which can be used equally well on its own or in a container, and is very useful in spaces were we might not normally be able to have flowers. Some spaces, although long are quite narrow, and florists' foam is a boon in such places. You don't always want your flower decoration to protrude too far into a room or intrude on your guests or family.

Baskets of flowers are relatively easy to make. All you need is a good basket, some of that florists' foam, and away you go, taking into account what we have already said about colour, size, symmetry and design. You can choose fresh flowers, dried flowers, or a mixture and work in lots of colour combinations to create the right effect. Remember to keep the foam moist if using fresh flowers.

*   *   *

In this chapter we have covered a lot of material connected with colour – what colours mean, which chakra centres they link to, and which flowers we may wish to consider in connection with both the chakra centres and meditation on colour. We have also discussed decorating the home with flowers of various colours. At this point, you may wish to experiment a little. Feel free. You do not need to finish reading the book before you start. Get going, and introduce more colour into your life and your surroundings by using flowers to their best advantage, but remember what we have learnt about colours and their subconscious meaning! In Chapter 3, we will take a look at the superstitions which have built up around the flowers over the centuries, worldwide.

SUPERSTITIONS, FOLKLORE, FLOWERS AND HERBS

In Chapter 1, we looked at the historical use of flowers and plants. Much of this gave rise to superstitions regarding the various flora around us, some of which have been handed down to us, often unquestioned.

In this chapter, we will be looking at some of these superstitions, how they came about, how they developed, and how they fit into today's culture.

SUPERSTITIONS IN THEIR PLACE

In the introduction to this book, I mentioned that my mother would not allow me to bring lilac into the house, because of the superstition that heavily scented flowers, of which lilac is one, were said to be the homes of dead souls. Bringing lilac into the house would, then, bring in death, especially if the lilac were white. In Belgium, lilac is often placed on a deathbed.

White flowers in general are associated with death by some cultures, because white was the ancient colour of mourning, and also whiteness was reminiscent of the pallor of death. For that reason, many people in several countries refuse to take the first white snowdrop of the season into the house because the flower is the colour of a shroud or burial gown. Likewise, the flower of the hawthorn tree, a white flower sometimes known as white may, was

considered to bring death into a house. If a child accidentally brought the flower into the house, it was thought at one time that the mother would die, and as a result many women will still not use the white may flower in home flower arrangements. Again this has a heavy scent, and its connection with white makes it a powerful omen. Another flower which it was said should not be brought into the house is the foxglove, although this has no noticeable scent, and is certainly not white. Similar thoughts apply to primroses, especially if only a single primrose is brought inside.

We were very keen in our family on lavender bags, which we kept in clothing drawers. In order to change our luck, we would seek to gather lavender when there was a new moon, and make three lavender bags, using muslin and silver cord knotted three times. The first bag would be put somewhere in the home, the second was carried around by one of us, and the third was given away to the first person we came across, as a present. We would also go outside to look at the new moon (not through glass as this was considered unlucky) and spat on a sixpence, which was then kept until the next new moon to help the luck of the family. My parents did this faithfully every new moon.

Another strange custom followed in my family was the keeping of a nutmeg about one's person, believed to protect the bearer from rheumatism. However, it didn't work for my father, and I leave you to make up your own mind as to whether this benefits you and your family.

I was told once that sage would help to improve my memory during exam time. Putting a sage leaf under my pillow would help me, or putting it in a book I was studying, would help me even more. If I left it there for four days and then applied it to my brow area, if I had studied well the knowledge contained in the book would be passed on to me, but if I hadn't studied or was considered unworthy, the sage leaf would erase the memory of anything I had tried to learn. I remember trying it out, but can't honestly say whether it worked, one way or the other. I do remember, however, taking a four-leaf clover into all my exams with me, in order to 'gain the help of the fairies'. Many people over the centuries have believed in fairies, and they also believed that fairies live in flowers.

fairies, pixies, elves and protection

Many people have linked flowers with elves, fairies, sprites and pixies. The ancient Britons thought that the foxglove was the hiding place of elves and fairies, while in Ireland it was thought that the bells of that flower provided tiny caps and petticoats for the fairies. Tulips were thought to be where fairies slept, and were known as fairies' cradles by many who shook the tulip before picking it to ensure that the fairies inside would escape. In Devon, people believed that the stitchwort was a special favourite of the pixies, and they thus always hesitated before picking stitchwort, just in case they should fall foul of a spell. Woodsorrel, with its bell-shaped flowers, was expected to ring like church bells to call the elves and fairies to any parties arranged.

In Grigson's *The Englishman's Flora*, there are 37 examples of the word 'fairy' in plant names. Some of these are cowslip (fairies' flower) and toadflax (fairies' lanterns). In Shakespeare's time, it was thought that the mottlings on the cowslip and foxglove were elves' fingerprints, and Shakespeare gave the cowslip to Puck as his home in *The Tempest*. Cowslips were thought to have got their name from their smell, which is said to resemble the smell of a cow's breath. The cuckoo flower, sometimes also known as lady's smock, is traditionally a fairy plant, and as such it is thought to be unlucky to bring it into the house. There are indeed many links with the names of flowers and fairies, from fairy bells to fairy caps. Conversely, there are also more than 50 species of flora which bear the name of Satan, including devil's blossom, devil daisy and devildums, and flowers called witch flowers and witch gowns.

WARDING OFF EVIL

In ancient Greece, it was thought that an anemone brought into the home would keep one free from evil forces and keep misfortune at a distance. Likewise, the peony root, one of the herbs connected with solar phenomena, was considered particularly effective as a

protection, as indeed were any flowers or plants which have associations with the sun. Consecrated by a magician on a Sunday, being the day of the sun, and carried in the pocket, the peony root would give peace of mind. The sunflower, which is also representative of the solar wheel, is often seen as a protection plant, and is also linked to Jesus because its head follows the light all day. Hazel branches, if collected on Palm Sunday and kept alive in water, were said to protect a household from lightning – in fact, there are many trees and bushes which offer the same protection. Many people in ancient times actively planned their gardens around certain flowers and trees for this reason. In addition to flowers already mentioned, other luck bringers include foxgloves (also known as fairy weeds), morning glory and marigolds, with periwinkles for health protection and marshmallows as a remedy against most diseases. It was, however, thought by some people that the souls of the dead lived in the foxglove, and also in thyme, and many people aware of this superstition would not grow foxgloves in their gardens, even if they also believed in fairies.

Planting lilies in the garden would keep away ghosts, although lily-of-the-valley was considered unlucky. Lilies generally, though, represent peace, calm and purity, so lilies, especially Madonna lilies, will help to create a calm and happy garden. Clover was also a fortunate plant to cultivate, as it was thought to keep away evil spirits. Trees which should be included in any garden hoping to attract fortune are the bay tree, an amulet against lightning, the oak and mountain ash which protect against witches, and the myrtle for a happy home life and children. Having ferns in the garden would also protect the home from thunder and lightning, as would the hawthorn tree and rosemary. Ferns always work well in a garden anyway, especially in a shady corner, where they can bring about a feeling of tranquillity. A rowan tree should also be planted in a garden to bring luck, and it was considered an ill omen to cut one down unless it became diseased or a danger to the fabric of the house.

To be sure that a house itself will be protected from witchcraft, one should think of growing ivy around the brickwork or mugwort in the garden. Should the ivy, however, suddenly fall away from the house, it is a sign that misfortune may be on the way in some form or

another. Many people also believed that ivy would prevent drunkenness, possibly due to the connection with Bacchus, mentioned in Chapter 1. To benefit from this protection, one should take a drink of vinegar in which ivy berries have been steeped, and failing that, once the drinking spree has ended, a drink made from ivy leaves would cure the hangover.

In Japan, the iris is thought to protect against evil spirits. Interestingly, the iris is also connected to the goddess of the same name who led the souls of women to their final resting place in the Underworld, protecting them from harm along the way.

Clover has long been considered an anti-witch plant, and possibly this gave rise to it being considered lucky, especially if it should have four leaves. This could enable the person concerned to detect witches and evil spirits, and so keep them free from troubles. Another plant connected with witches, Satan, demons and the dark forces was hemlock, as indeed were many other poisonous plants, such as henbane which was said to make children go to sleep and never wake up.

Hemlock was thought to be a plant used to anoint the body and aid flight, and it was once believed that if children should accidentally touch the hemlock plant, they would be taken away by the devil. In similar vein, the nightshade was also thought to be a plant used by witches to aid flight, bring death or hallucinations, if used sparingly. However, wearing a crown of nightshade leaves around the head would protect against witches and their spells, and for this reason nightshade was also put around the necks and heads of cattle, as was bittersweet.

Thunder plants

Poppies were often called red petticoats by many, and were thought to have special powers over thunder and lightning. In fact there were several plants which were given the quality of summoning up, or protecting against, thunder and lightning. Not surprisingly, these plants have been given the overall name of thunder plants. Some

people suggest that picking poppies, sometimes also called lightnings or thunderclap, would cause a storm to start, while others say that the poppy protects a house from lightning if picked and placed amongst the eaves. Other plants which are supposed to keep people safe during thunderstorms and which protect them and their property from lightning include the bugle, known in Gloucestershire as the thunder and lightning, the germander, known in Northamptonshire as the strikefire, and the house leek, known as syngreen by many and as Jupiter's plant to the Greeks because it was thought to protect from thunderbolts. It is considered to be very ill fortune to cut down the house leek in the West Country of England, where it is still known as Jupiter's beard, and it is said that the juices extracted from its leaves can make a soothing ointment in the treatment of burns and scalds. If, however, there is insufficient time to press the juices from the leaves, they can be placed intact on the wound and bound to the problem area.

In Kent, however, protection from thunderbolts was thought to come from the bladder campion, which also protected against snakes, while others thought that if the white-flowered stonecrop grew upon the roof it would protect a house from fire and lightning. The orpine, also called the live-long because it is long lasting, is another plant thought to protect against lightning and disease, but only if gathered on Midsummer's Eve and hung up immediately in the house concerned.

Nettles were also thought to protect against thunder, and if carried by a person would also protect the bearer against lightning and any other dangerous event.

Christendom's superstitious past

In an attempt to get more people involved in Christianity and away from paganism, many pagan traditions were actively employed by the early Christian Church based in Rome, and pagan festivals

merged with those of Christendom to attract a greater following. It should be no surprise, therefore, to realise that various flowers were also used by the Christian Church, which formerly had pagan associations, and these flowers are still used in many cases. Some have already been mentioned in Chapter 1 in connection with festivals, but other flowers were also brought into the Christian tradition from the ancient past. Flowers which were linked previously to Greek gods soon became linked with biblical names, such as Eve's cushion, Eve's tears, Mary bud, and so on. The cowslip is also sometimes called herb Peter, after the apostle Peter, because it is said the flowers of the cowslip resemble the bunch of keys that Peter holds at the gates of Heaven.

Some stories and legends about flowers have no basis in fact but owe their origins to fantasy. Legend, for example, says the snowdrop's origins resulted from Adam and Eve being cast out of the Garden of Eden. The story says that snow fell, the world was lifeless, but as a sign that things would improve, and that life, although not everlasting life, would continue for the couple, an angel breathed on the falling snow, and when this touched the ground, snowdrops sprang up on the spot. As a result of this legend, it was popularly supposed that the appearance of snowdrops was a promise of better things to come. Snowdrops are also connected to Mary, the link being the purity of the flower and the colour white, and there are, in fact, many plants known by names incorporating Mary or lady in the title.

Lilies are mentioned in the Bible in the Song of Solomon, and therefore the early Christians used the lily in artwork to indicate one of the greatest pleasures of paradise. The iris is linked with the Virgin Mary, and is called the flower of the Virgin, while the rose, once a flower dedicated to Venus and to love, became an expression of Christ's passion. The acanthus is another of the flowers of paradise, and is depicted in a thirteenth-century mosaic at St Clements in Rome, with the central theme of the impalement of Christ. Lilies-of-the-valley became linked to Mary, and were known in certain areas as Our Lady's tears, due to the story suggesting that they first sprang up where Mary's tears fell upon the death on her son. Lilies-of-the-valley were also linked to St Leonard, as they were supposed to have

bloomed first when his blood was shed during a three-day fight with a dragon at St Leonard's Forest.

Any plant with three leaves became associated with the Trinity, and that is one of the reasons why the Shamrock is so important to the Irish. Heartsease was also named herb Trinity.

At one time, it was also popular to believe that the red spots on the leaves of the St John's wort symbolised the blood of John the Baptist, and tradition suggested these spots would appear every year on the anniversary of his death, said to be 27 August. St John had, in fact, many plants associated with him – fennel, bracken, male fern, orpine, ivy, plantain, daisy, vervain, corn marigold, mugwort and yarrow.

FLOWERS AND PLANTS ASSOCIATED WITH CHRIST

The juniper tree saved the life of Jesus, according to several stories, during the flight into Egypt. It is said that Herod's men, close to discovering Jesus, failed to look in the juniper bush where he had been hidden, confirming the protective qualities of the tree.

Stems of the bracken plant, when cut crosswise close to the ground have certain marks upon them which were at one time thought to resemble the Greek letter Chi (X), which is also the first letter in the Greek form of Christ's name. As a result, witches and evil spirits were formerly thought to hate the bracken and would actively avoid anybody carrying it or standing near it. However, others possibly unaware of this link with Christ, albeit tenuous, thought that the initials seen on the cut stems would indicate the initials of the person they were likely to marry.

Holly, mentioned in connection with various festivals in Chapter 1, was also thought to have sprung up on the spot where Jesus first appeared after his death. The planting of holly was supposed not only to protect against evil, but also against bother by tax collectors. A similar story suggests that vervain was first found growing at the spot where Jesus died, and that it was used to help ease the pain

associated with his loss of blood. As such, vervain is sometimes called the holy herb.

We learnt in Chapter 1 how holly is principally connected with the Christian festival of Christmas celebrating Christ's birth. Many superstitions surround holly at Christmas time. It is said that when the branches of holly are laden with berries, a hard, cold winter is likely. Stamping on a holly berry is considered exceptionally unlucky, as is bringing the plant indoors when it is flowering in some areas of Britain. It is said that, when decorating a home for Christmas, the holly should be hung up before the mistletoe. This protects the family from ill luck and quarrels, especially over the festivities. It should also be picked before Christmas Eve, otherwise you might fall foul of evil intent by others. If after Twelfth Night holly is left up, this is a bad omen. Holly branches should be burnt on the hearth (if there is one) according to many superstitions, although what people with central heating do is not recorded! Other superstitions suggest, however, that burning the branches is not a good idea, and they must be thrown away and left to wither. Similarly, if the holly is thrown away too soon, it is thought to bring about a death in the family during the coming year. Another Christmas superstition suggests that it is unlucky to bring evergreens into a house before Christmas Eve, for this would seek to anticipate the festivities to come.

Many varied trees and bushes were linked with Christ's crown of thorns: some of these we have already mentioned. Roses were also linked with Jesus, and there are those who believe that the crown of thorns was made from rose briars. Following on from this is the thought that the rose, originally white, was stained when Christ's blood fell to the ground, and red roses sprang up where previously white roses had grown. Another story changes the flower to the scarlet pimpernel. Other plants linked to the place where Jesus died are the plant known as calvery clover, which has red spots on its leaves and a seedpod resembling the crown of thorns. Periscaria also has spots of red on its leaves.

The hawthorn is another plant linked with Christ, as is the elder, as being the two possible woods from which the torture stake on which Jesus died was made, and it is again interesting that the hawthorn was also considered a holy tree in pagan times, unlike the elder in

whose branches witches were supposed to live. It is said that the elder tree is the one that Judas chose to hang himself from after the betrayal, although this is unlikely.

Roses became linked to the Christian tradition, and were dedicated to Mary and considered a symbol of virginity. The lungwort's blue flowers are said to be Mary's eyes, the red buds her eyelids, wet with tears, while the pale spots on the leaves show where her tears fell at the death of her son. As a result, this plant is sometimes called Mary's tears.

The crown imperial is connected to the Easter tradition. It is suggested that the plant refused to bow its head when Jesus passed by on the way to his death. The flower was thus cursed to hang its head in shame, with a tear of sorrow at the centre of each petal. The passion flower, named after the passion of Christ, was said to represent the spear that wounded Jesus, the upright column of the ovary representing the torture stake itself. The stamens are likened to the nails that were used to pierce the hands and feet and the five petals represent the five wounds. The crown of thorns was represented by the dark circle in the centre of the flower. Should the flower be blue in colour, it was thought to represent Heaven, whereas if it were white, this was symbolic of purity. The flower has a three-day life only, symbolising the three days that Jesus lay in the tomb.

The changing of a flower's colours follows through in the Christian tradition with the story of the rosemary, whose flowers were also white originally. Again, during the flight into Egypt, legend suggests that Mary spread Jesus's clothes to dry on a rosemary bush, the flowers turned blue and have remained so to this day. Another such legend tells that the plant grows only for 33 years (the age at which Jesus died), until it reaches the height at which Jesus died. After that, it will no longer grow upwards, but outwards.

Superstitions associated with the devil

The devil also had various plants associated with him. Early Christians believed that the garlic plant and the wormwood plant sprang up

from the devil's footprints when he was originally cast from Heaven. Likewise the mandrake was closely associated with the devil, and often called 'devil's plant' or 'devil's apples'. It was said to grow only where the fluids from the body of a hanged man had fallen to the ground. There were many plants prefixed by the name devil at one time; such names as devil's bit, old man's beard and the like were once quite commonplace. The common parsley is also associated with the devil.

Other superstitions

Death, illness and bad luck

Many people will not put white and red flowers in the same vase because they are symbolic of 'blood and bandages'. In fact, some hospital nurses separate the red and white flowers as it is said that a death will result in the ward, although this may not necessarily be the death of the patient for whom the flowers were originally intended. Similarly, actors are known to try to prevent real flowers being used on stage, as they are supposed to bring bad luck to the play, although it is acceptable for actresses to be presented with bouquets after a performance!

It is said that any flower which blooms out of season is a death omen, and that white flowers which wilt on being brought into a house also foretell of death. Dreaming of white flowers is also considered a death omen by some people. Likewise, it is considered bad fortune to bring snowdrops into a house, especially if one single flower is brought in because a death may follow. This superstition seems to owe its roots to the fact that the snowdrop grows close to the ground, and as such remains close to the grave and the dead. It is also white, which for many, as we know from Chapter 1, is associated with death.

Parsley, at one time, was used as a garland, and given to the victors at the Nemean Games. As an evergreen it was also used by Romans

to line the graves of the dead. Sowing parsley has since come to mean a death in the family within the next 12 months, unless this is done on Good Friday, and it is also thought that transplanting parsley will give your garden to the devil, although the Good Friday connection will protect you here, as well. If someone offers you some parsley, you may choose to accept it by all means, but never give it away yourself, as it is thought you will also be giving away your luck.

Flowers often acquired their names from people. The forget-me-not is said to have acquired its name from the medieval knight who, dying from battle wounds, threw the flower to his loved one with the words 'forget me not'. Since then the flower has been called by the name as a mark of respect. Likewise, the narcissus is said to be named after the vain young man of the same name who fell in love with his own reflection, and pined to death. Following on from this comes the superstition that the perfume of this flower will cause madness.

Narcissus

Roses are normally associated with love, but this is not always the case. In Germany, it was considered that putting rose petals on the fire would bring luck, but in England it was thought unlucky to drop rose petals on the floor as this would bring the angel of death into the home. Even dropping petals from roses being carried or worn upon the person has long been considered unlucky, and like many flowers, it is considered unlucky when a rose blooms out of season.

To dream of roses has always been considered good fortune for love, unless the flower is white, in which case it may connect, again, with death.

Roses were also considered symbolic of silence, dedicated to Harpocrates the god of silence, and as such were used in church ceiling decorations, and also in the halls of grand places, especially in Germany, where officials from government would meet. It was once traditional, if you wanted to talk freely without fear that your story would be retold elsewhere, to wear a garland of roses around your neck.

In many places, it is common to find bushes planted in the memory of a loved one who has died. Gardens of remembrance often contain roses, and in certain places, the colour of the roses planted is an indication of the person buried. White roses were often planted in memory of virgins, while red roses showed respect for someone who was of good character and nature. Red roses were also commonly planted on the graves of lovers, normally at the head of the grave.

It was customary at one time for a man who had been deserted by his lover, either in death or from another cause, to wear a garland of willow flowers. It was also customary for someone who had been jilted to receive a garland of willow flowers when the errant partner married someone else.

Violets are thought to be unlucky if brought into a house in small quantities, and used as love charms when put into salads, made into jams and cordials and given to prospective mates to aid the course of true love.

Catkins are also thought to be unlucky by many if brought into a house, but if they are picked and brought in on May Day morning they are lucky and will protect the household for the coming 12 months.

The mugwort was often carried by travellers in the Middle Ages as a protection against tiredness on the journey, a belief which can also be found within Roman superstition. Another plant capable protecting against witchcraft and evil, the mugwort was also thought to protect against thunder.

Lilies, associated with purity, are often thought to spring up on the graves of men who have been executed for a crime of which they were, in truth, innocent. Popular with many for use at weddings because of their link with purity, they are also used at funerals, and some people will not accept them into their homes because of the latter association. Likewise, many will not accept meadowsweet into the home, as it is said the fragrance will bring about a deep sleep from which you may never awaken. Again, this links to the fact that the meadowsweet has a heady smell, as does the lilac mentioned in Chapter 1.

Poppies were often felt to protect the cornfield in which they grew from ill effect, and were actively associated with fertility. In some areas it is considered ill luck to bring poppies into the house, because they would bring illness to the family. In modern times, however, the poppy has become associated with remembrance of war victims, because of the growth of poppies on the battlefields of Flanders, and as such artificial poppies are worn by those people who wish to remember those killed during warfare and battles, especially on Remembrance Day (11 November). The poppy is also connected to Jesus Christ in that the red symbolises the blood He shed and the cross in the centre is symbolic of the resurrection.

Prior to the poppy, rosemary was the plant linked with remembrance. Rosemary is also considered a symbol of fidelity in love. Before newly married couples partook of the wedding feast, it was customary at one time for sprigs of rosemary to be dipped into the wine, as a protection and to ensure continuing happiness. It was also used at funerals and planted at the graveside in many places, again to ensure remembrance. Rosemary is still worn by Australians on their hats on Anzac Day as a symbol of remembrance.

Love

Sorrel, it is said, helps to bring peace between a quarrelling couple, and causes love to grow between two people if served to them in a soup.

The orpine, also known as midsummer men, was used on Midsummer Eve to establish if a lover was true. It was cut and fixed in clay upon a

shell, slate or crack in the door, and if on the following morning the stalk were leaning to the right, the girl's lover was true. If, however, it leaned to the left, he was false. Another superstition was to bring in two pieces of orpine, and if they bent together, the couple's love would blossom. However, if they bent away from each other, there would be no marriage. If one or other of the stalks died, it suggested one of the partners would die before too long. Another plant used on Midsummer's Eve was the sage. If a young person wanted to know his or her future mate, it was necessary to pick twelve leaves at midnight on Midsummer Eve, or also on St Mark's Eve, pulling one for each note of the striking clock, and taking care to ensure the leaf be pulled whole from the stem. The person would then see the future mate, either in person or in a dream. Incidentally, many flowers became linked to Midsummer, and it was customary at one time to decorate houses with lilies, birch, fennel, orpine and St John's wort at the time of the Midsummer festivities, it being thought that any flowers picked at that time would last better than others.

Mint was thought to help virility in men, and a man seeking to increase his virility was advised to carry a sprig of mint and drink copious amounts of mint tea. Likewise, a woman wishing to increase her fertility should gather lemon balm.

The periwinkle is often believed to have the power to create love, and as such can be used in rituals aimed at attracting lovers. One such folklore suggests powdering periwinkles with earthworms to be eaten with meat as an aphrodisiac. If you wish to try this, please do so, but don't ask me to share the meal! As mentioned earlier, the periwinkle was also called the flower of death in Italy, and used to make garlands for dead babies, while in France during the Middle Ages it was connected with death when it was used as a garland for those on their way to execution. It is also said be unlucky to dig up a periwinkle found growing in a grave. However, it is thought by most to be a love plant, rather than anything else.

The cyclamen, if made into cakes and eaten, is supposed to act as a love potion and was a powerful aphrodisiac in days gone by. It was also thought that if the myrtle bloomed during any one season, someone in the household would marry. The myrtle is said to grow

best if planted by a woman, and it was felt that drinking an infusion made from the leaves would increase the beauty of the person concerned. If such an infusion were offered by a lover to his partner, it was thought that love would be retained and everlasting. A similar thought revolved around the giving of a flowering sprig of myrtle. It was further thought, in some areas, that if a young girl took a sprig of myrtle on Midsummer Eve, and placed it in her prayer book at the part dealing with the marriage service, then slept with it under her pillow, should the myrtle be gone in the morning, her lover would marry her. However, if the myrtle remained, strangely it meant that her lover would not marry her.

The myrtle and rosemary flowers were often used by brides in their wedding bouquets, but the use of orange blossom is now far more popular. Many brides will have this blossom in their bouquets unaware of the superstition that it was a love charm and would bring children into a marriage.

In medieval times, wallflowers were worn as badges by knights as a sign to everybody that they intended to remain faithful to their lady. Strangely, today, wallflowers seem to be connected to those people who don't want to join in any fun.

Most women will also, at some time or another, have seen others, or tried themselves, pulling the petals off a daisy one by one, and reciting alternately 'he loves me, he loves me not'. It is thought possible to discover, when the last petal is pulled, how one stands with one's prospective lover. How many of us, however, would admit to having thrown away one flower, and given it another go, when we don't get the answer we want! It was also thought that dreaming of marigolds would lead to a prosperous and happy marriage.

If a quarrel had occurred with a loved one, it was considered that Midsummer Day was the day to patch things up, as mentioned previously. By gathering a bunch of marigolds or marshmallows at dusk, and placing them in silence in a jug of water on an outside windowsill, it was thought that the wanderer would return home within three weeks. Special flowers for Midsummer's Day include St John's wort, lady's slipper, vervain, wild laburnum and scarlet lychnis. It was thought that at midnight on 24 June, St John's Day, anybody finding a

flower from this group in bloom would also have everlasting happiness. Similarly, it was thought that the giving of violets showed true love.

Valerian is another plant thought to help in matters of the heart, and was considered to have aphrodisiac qualities. In some areas, it was thought that a lady who carried with her a sprig of valerian would have plenty of suitors, but as the smell of the flowers is not terribly pleasant, we may now wonder why!

If a girl wanted to get her lover back to her, she could, by using the rose. Three roses needed to be gathered, again on Midsummer's Eve, one of which had to be buried in the small hours of Midsummer morning under a yew tree, another in a newly made grave, and the third put under the girl's pillow. If the rose was left under the pillow for three days and then burnt, the girl would haunt her lover's dreams until, unable to take anymore, he returned to her.

FINDING A MATE

It was thought that if a young girl put a sprig of mistletoe under her pillow on Midsummer night, she would dream of her future husband, although in parts of Austria, it was believed that mistletoe would merely deliver a person from nightmares. Cowslips, it was once thought, could also be used to help find the name of a future husband. By making the flowers into a ball, the girl should toss the ball into the air, saying 'Titsy, tosty, tell me true, who shall I be married to?' She should then shout out all the names of the men she had desires towards, and the ball would fall to the ground when the right name was shouted. The hempseed could also be used with the ditty 'hempseed I sow, hempseed, grow, he that is to marry me, come after me and mow'. It was assumed that if the hempseed were thrown over the left shoulder at midnight in a churchyard and the ditty spoken, an image of the girl's future husband would appear, mowing the area with a scythe. Should nothing happen, it was assumed that the girl would remain single for a least a year, but should a coffin be seen instead of a man in the vision, she would die unmarried and young.

The yarrow was also employed as an inducement to dream of a future mate, but only if taken from the grave of a recently deceased young man, and then immediately placed under the pillow of the young person and a rhyme repeated. A similar superstition surrounds the yew. This could be picked from anywhere in the churchyard, but it should be one never before visited.

In certain parts of Britain it was believed that if a young woman put an ivy leaf in her pocket, the first man she met when out walking would marry her, even if he were already married. It would happen eventually, and she should be patient. Likewise, if a spinster put ivy under her pillow on 21 December, St Thomas's Day, having prayed to St Thomas, she would then dream of her future husband. Dreaming of ivy was, in any event, considered to be very lucky and to foretell happiness. Other stories suggest that, in France, a gentleman who admired a lady from a distance should find the tiniest ivy leaf he could and bind it with a single, pale blue silk thread and tie this into a little bow. He should then send it, anonymously, to the lady in question. It was felt that the smaller the ivy leaf used, the greater his love would be.

Rosemary was thought to help a young girl dream of her husband. A sprig of rosemary and a silver sixpence under her pillow on All Hallow's Eve would guarantee such a dream. If, however, she placed a plate of flour under a rosemary bush on Midsummer's Eve, she would find her husband's initials written in the flour. The four-leafed clover, mentioned earlier in connection with protection from evil was also thought, if worn in the right shoe by a young girl, to guarantee her meeting her future husband, who was normally the first man she would then come across, or another man of the same name.

GOOD FORTUNE

It was thought that to cut a fern, or to burn it, would bring rain, and this could be actively used at times when rain was needed by farmers. However, it is said that Charles I, aware of this, suggested to Lord Pembroke that he issue orders that no fern be burnt in Staffordshire during the time of his visit in 1636, as he wanted fine weather.

Another superstition connected to the fern suggested that fernseed, which would make one invisible, could also enable a suitor to summon up any creature on earth, which could help him with his courting. Conversely, a man might consider putting fernseed in his shoes, which again, making him invisible, could help him to discover hidden treasures and acquire wealth, which would certainly then help his chances with the ladies. Gathering the fernseed, however, had to be done on Midsummer's Eve between the hours of 11 p.m. and midnight, and the seeds had to be gathered without them being touched.

The chicory plant was also thought to have the power to make people invisible, and also shared with springwort, vervain and moonwort the gift of being able to unlock doors and boxes, but only if the plant were gathered at noon or midnight on St James' Day (25 July).

*　　*　　*

In this chapter we have looked at many superstitions involving plants and flowers, and how some of these have survived, while others are lost in myth. Many superstitions have been merely kept alive by transferring an existing story into a Christian context to give it more credence, and many more have continued to live because we have failed to question them, but accepted them as part and parcel of our daily lives. There are more superstitions connected with flowers and plants which I do not have space to include, but I hope you will be inspired to do your own further research.

In the next chapter, we will look at the Victorians' attitude to flowers, as it was during this period that flower symbolism or what became known as 'the language of flowers' was formed.

ThE LaNGUAGE
OF FLOWERS

In Chapter 2 we looked at the use of flowers and colour, and you will have noted that the Victorians, passionate about flowers, used them not only as decoration around the home, but also in paintings and fabric design, as well as in dress and hat design. Possibly because of the intense interest in flowers which was aroused during the period, a 'language of flowers' developed. In this chapter, we will discuss this is greater detail, seeing where some of the thoughts as to the meanings of the flowers originated. We will also take a look at dreams of flowers, and the traditional meanings associated with these.

Our Love affair with flowers

To many, the rose will forever be the flower of love, and will probably always be given by people as a sign of affection. Interestingly, prior to the rose becoming the symbol of love and affection, the tulip was the flower of love until the Middle Ages or shortly thereafter. Tulips, which possibly originated in Turkey and then were brought to the Netherlands in the 1590s, were a very hot commodity by the 1630s when they were highly prized and very valuable, and it was not unusual, in the Netherlands, for a bride's dowry to be paid in the form of a tulip bulb, while three bulbs would be the price for a canalside house.

Flowers have always been used to convey affection, and the language of flowers became something which would help to conceal the actual meaning of the gift from those who were not privy to the secret knowledge. To the Victorian lady, receiving a flower could be quite a thrill. An admirer had to follow strict codes of etiquette demanded by the conventions of Victorian society, so particular flowers were chosen for the 'message' they conveyed. The lady concerned would consult the literature available at the time to discover the intent of the admirer, and reply accordingly. All this was carried out with the utmost discretion and a certain amount of secrecy. Many florists even today will be aware of the traditional meanings of various flowers, and can advise customers which flowers convey what messages. Many people, however, will stick to the rose, knowing that if all else fails, the message of love will still get through, although the colour might be an important factor.

Before we look at the Victorians though, we should be aware that there have always been traditions linking flowers with particular meanings and with particular months.

Month	Flower	Meaning
January	Narcissus	Self-love
February	Iris	Hope
March	Daffodil	Chivalry
April	Daisy	Innocence
May	Iris	Primeval fire
June	Rose	Feminine beauty
July	Cornflower	Delicacy
August	Dahlia	Dignity
September	Gladioli	Protection
October	Aster	Truth
November	Violet	Union of body and spirit
December	Carnation	Divine love

Following on from this, the days of the week also have flowers traditionally associated with them. Some people believe that good luck will follow them if they stick to the flower for the day, or the flower belonging to the day on which they were born. You may wish to try this out for yourself.

Sunday Any flower which is golden or orange coloured, after the colour of the sun – this day of the week being the sun's day. Day lilies, sunflowers, pot marigolds, certain varieties of primrose, yellow tulip, gaillardia, California poppies, golden rod, monbretia, yellow irises and doronicum are flowers for this day.

Monday Any flower which is white or silver is appropriate in this day, which is named after the moon – anything which, therefore, relates to the moon is considered acceptable. Honesty, pearl everlasting, star of Bethlehem, common white jasmine, lily-of-the-valley, moon daisies, white roses, white canterbury bells, snowdrops or scented white phlox are the flowers for this day. Mistletoe, with its berries often being thought to resemble the moon, might also be considered.

Phlox

Tuesday Linked to Mars and thus to anything red, the flowers for this day are scarlet nasturtiums, dahlias, geraniums, oriental poppies, red-hot pokers (kniphofia) and any red-berried plant, such as holly or flame-red glory flowers.

Wednesday This is the day with which rainbow-coloured flowers are associated, together with any flowers which link with communication, such as the iris, known as the messenger to the gods. Other flowers to consider include lupins, columbines, salpiglosis, night-scented stock and vervain. You could also look at

plants which have multi-coloured leaves or flowers which contain several colours within them, such as certain types of sweet William.

Thursday Any flower which is blue or mauve belongs to this day, so lilac, lavender, violets, stocks, cyclamen, foxglove, delphinium, larkspur, catmint and blazing star are all to be considered.

Friday Connected to love, because of its association with Venus, any flower which is pink or light blue is associated with this day. Consequently, you might consider pinks, carnations, pink roses, forget-me-nots, African lily, masterwort, Peruvian lily or Michaelmas daisies. Other choices could possibly be pink or blue verbena.

Saturday Connected with Saturn and with brown and dark reds, bronze chrysanthemums, dahlias and wallflowers are associated with this day, as are varieties of Mexican aster.

What the Victorians had to say

The Victorian system of flower language may have its roots way back in the sands of time, but there is no concrete evidence, and we can only hypothesise. Irrespective of flower meanings or thoughts on their meanings, a flower is an expression of sentiment in its own right. However, it has not always been the case that one could send flowers to an admirer, friend or loved one with the ease that there is today. There are many times in our history when it has not been possible for people to be 'up front' with their affections, and a certain amount of decorum was dictated by society as a whole. Often messages of love were sent from one person to another using an intermediary, so that a distance could be observed and irate parents may not get to know the full story behind the gift. If such gifts were intercepted, anonymity preserved the dignity of the persons involved.

Unfortunately, sometimes this little game would go horribly wrong, when the gift might be received by the wrong person, or someone

could deliberately seek to deceive another by the giving of a gift. Likewise, it would be possible for someone skilled in the knowledge of the meaning of the various flowers to substitute one flower for another, or conversely for the florist to confuse the flowers, or on finding difficulty getting one flower, substitute another, thus changing the meaning completely and giving a false message.

If you wish to start using this 'secret language' be sure you know exactly what each flower means. If you are making up a bouquet, check out *all* the flowers you are intending to use, and make sure that the recipient gets the information on the meaning of flowers well beforehand, so that he or she, too, is able to interpret the message correctly. Think also in terms of colours, and do be sure, irrespective of the message, to give a bouquet where the colours and sizes of the blooms match and are appropriate, and the overall effect is one of beauty, as well as of intrigue!

Aconite   Dislike. 'Your attentions are not welcome.'
Agrimony   Thanks. 'Accept my thanks for your gift.'
Almond, flowering   Hope. 'Your friendship is enjoyable.'
Alyssum   Virtue and worthiness. 'I admire your noble character.'
Amaryllis   Pride. 'I would be proud to have you as my friend.'
Anemone   Estrangement. 'I no longer find you attractive.'
Angelica   Inspiration. 'You inspire me to great things.'
Apple blossom   Beauty and goodness, with temptations. 'I find you beautiful.'
Arbutus   Love. 'You are my only true love.'
Arum, wild   Passion. 'I am burning with desire for you.'
Asphodel   Mourning. 'My love remains even though you are no longer with me.'
Aster   Regrets. 'I regret my rashness. Please do not take me too seriously.'
Azalea   Moderation. 'Please be less impetuous and moderate your actions.'
Balm   Fun. 'I was only joking with you.'
Balsam   Impatience. 'I am counting the time, 'til we meet again.'
Barberry   Hot temper. 'You should watch your anger.'
Basil   Animosity. 'I dislike you.'

Beeorchid   Misunderstanding. 'You have misjudged both me and my actions.'
Begonia   Warning. 'Our love is no longer a secret. We are being watched.'
Bellflower   Morning time. 'Meet me tomorrow morning.'
Bindweed, greater   Persistence. 'I cannot, as yet, accept you.'
Bindweed, lesser   Humility. 'I am deeply sorry, and seek your forgiveness.'
Bird's foot trefoil   Retribution. 'You are fickle, and will reap what you sow.'
Bittersweet   Truth. 'I am sincere in both word and action.'
Blackthorn   Obstacles. 'There are problems in our path.'
Bluebell   Constancy. 'I am faithful, always.'
Bluebottle   Celibacy. 'While I would like to get to know you, I am afraid to do so.'
Borage   Brusqueness. 'I do not like you and wish you would get away from me.'
Bracken   Enchantment.   'I am fascinated by you.'
Bramble   Remorse. 'I am sorry if I acted too quickly, and seek your forgiveness.'
Broom   Devotion. 'I am forever yours.'
Buckbean   Rest. 'May you sleep peacefully.'
Bugloss   Untruthful. 'You are false.'
Bulrush   Rashness. 'Please be more discreet.'
Burdock   Persistence. 'I will not give up.'
Buttercup   Radiance. 'You are beautiful.'
Cactus   No. 'I have no interest in you, at all.'
Camellia   Loveliness. 'You are lovely.'
Camomile   Fortitude. 'I admire your courage and strength. Keep going.'
Campion, meadow   Poverty. 'I am only poor, and yet I admire you.'
Campion, red   Encouragement. 'I should like to get to know you.'
Campion, white   Evening. 'Meet me at nightfall.'
Canterbury bell, blue   Faithfulness. 'I do love you, truly.'
Canterbury bell, white   Acknowledgement. 'I got your gift, and will treasure it.'
Carnation, pink   Encouragement. 'Thank you for your gift.'

Carnation, red   Passionate love. 'I love you, and must see you soon.'
Carnation, white   Purity of affection. 'I love you with purity of heart.'
Celandine, lesser   Reawakening. 'I still love you.'
Cherry blossom   Increase. 'May our friendship blossom.'
Chrysanthemum, bronze   Friendship. 'I value you as a friend only.'
Chrysanthemum, red   Reciprocated love. 'I love you.'
Chrysanthemum, yellow   Discouragement. 'I love someone else.'
Chrysanthemum, white   Truth. 'I believe in you, and speak the truth.'
Cineraria   Delight. 'I find you good company.'
Cinquefoil   Sisterly affection. 'I regard you as a brother.'
Cistus   Favour. 'You are the most beautiful of women I know.'
Clarkia   Pleasure. 'I enjoy your company and your conversation.'
Cleavers   Tenacity. 'Whatever it takes, I will win your love.'
Clematis   Intellectuality. 'I have beautiful thoughts of you, and admire your mind.'
Clover, pink   Injured pride. 'Do not trifle with me anymore.'
Clover, red   Petition. 'Even though we are apart, will you remain faithful?'
Clover, white   Promise. 'I will be true to you.'
Columbine, purple   Resolve. 'I shall never give you up.'
Columbine, white   Foolishness. 'I was stupid to be so forward with you.'
Convolvulus   Mistakes. 'I am not totally yours.'
Coreopsis   Love at first sight. 'I am totally lost in love with you.'
Coriander   Hidden value. 'Do not judge me by my appearance alone.'
Cornflower   Delicacy. 'Take your time, and don't rush me so much.'
Crocus, spring   Happiness. 'My heart and yours are as one, but don't abuse me.'
Currant, flowering   Presumption. 'You have assumed too much. We are not alike at all.'
Cyclamen   Indifference. 'I am not bothered by you one way or the other.'
Daffodil   Diffidence. 'I am shy, and do not totally return your affections.'

Dahlia, red   Rebuff. 'You are wrong in your assumptions on my feelings for you.'
Dahlia, white   Dismissal. 'Keep away from me. You are unstable.'
Dahlia, yellow   Distaste. 'I do not like you in any way at all.'

Dahlia

Daisy, field   Delay. 'I am unable to reply to you for a while.'
Daisy, Michaelmas   Goodbye. 'Don't try to contact me as I can never love you.'
Daisy, ox-eye   Hope. 'Given time, I might come to love you.'
Dandelion   Absurdity. 'I find you totally ridiculous.'
Deadly nightshade   Deception. 'You are not what you pretend to be.'
Deadnettle, red   Coolness. 'You have upset me.'
Deadnettle, white   Coolness. 'I do not like you.'
Dogrose   Loveliness. 'You are as lovely as this flower.'
Dogviolet   Enthralment. 'You are my first love.'
Enchanter's nightshade   Double dealing. 'Don't cheat me.'
Evening primrose   Quiet devotion. 'I adore you.'
Everlasting flower   Death of hope. 'You have sent me away, but I shall always love you and will never forget you.'
Feverfew   Protection. 'I will look after you.'
Flax, blue   Thanks. 'You are more than kind.'
Flax, red   Appreciation. 'I deeply appreciate your love.'
Fleur de lys   Passion. 'I burn with love for you.'
Fool's parsley   Folly. 'Don't be silly, for we can still be friends.'

Forget-me-not   Remembrance. 'Think of me when we are apart, for my love is true.'

Foxglove   Shallowness. 'You do not really love me at all.'

Fuchsia   Warning. 'Be careful, because the person you love is not true to you.'

Gardenia   Sweetness. 'You are pure and untouched.'

Geranium, pink   Doubt. 'Please explain yourself to me.'

Geranium, red   Duplicity. 'I cannot and do not trust you.'

Geranium, white   Indecision. 'I am not sure, and need time to make up my mind.'

Gilliflower   Affection. 'You are very important to me.'

Gladiolus   Pain. 'What you said has really upset me. I may be prepared to discuss this.'

Golden rod   Indecision. 'I have not decided yet.'

Harebell   Resignation. 'I accept what you say, but will still live in hope.'

Hawthorn   Hope. 'Regardless of what you say, I will still try to win your heart.'

Heliotrope   Devotion. 'You are the only reason for my living.'

Hellebore   Lies. 'Don't believe what others tell you about me. I can explain.'

Hemlock   Scandal. 'I have been accused falsely.'

Hepatica   Confidence. 'I trust you implicitly.'

Hollyhock   Ambition. 'I could achieve anything with you by my side.'

Honesty   Frankness. 'I have been totally honest with you. You know everything.'

Honeysuckle   Betrothal. 'I give you all that I am, and all that I have.'

Hyacinth, blue   Devotion. 'I would lay down my life for you, if it were asked.'

Hyacinth, white   Admiration. 'I admire you.'

Hydrangea   Changeableness. 'Why are you so fickle?'

Iris   Ardour. 'I feel a great deal for you in my heart.'

Ivy   Bonds. 'Will you marry me?'

Jasmine   Elegance. 'You are elegant beyond words.'

Jasmine, cape   Hope. 'Better times will come for us.'

Jonquil   Appeal. 'May I hope that you might love me, eventually?'

Laburnum   Neglect. 'Why have you left me?'

Larkspur Trifling. 'Don't mess with my emotions any more. Let me know.'

Lavender Refusal. 'While I like you a lot, I don't love you, as I mistrust you.'

Lilac, purple First love. 'You are my first love.'

Lilac, white Innocence. 'You are beautiful, and my spirits are moved by you.'

Lily, tiger Passion. 'I cannot hold myself back from loving you.'

Lily, white Purity. 'I feel overwhelmed by your purity.'

Lily-of-the-valley Friendship. 'Be my friend. Don't talk to me of love.'

Lobelia, blue Dislike. 'I neither like you or love you, nor ever could.'

Lobelia, white Rebuff. 'You are wrong in your assumptions about my emotions for you.'

London pride Flirtation. 'I am sorry if I flirted with you, but it was only in fun. I do not find you attractive.'

Loosestrife, purple Apologies. 'I am sorry. Please take this as a peace offering.'

Loosestrife, yellow Peace. 'Let's forget our argument. I am sorry.'

Love in a mist Uncertainty. 'I don't understand your message. What do you mean?'

Love lies bleeding Broken heart. 'My life is empty if you refuse to see me.'

Lupin Overboldness. 'Stop being so pushy, and I might change my mind.'

Magnolia Strength. 'Don't give up. Better days are coming.'

Marigold, African Lack of attraction. 'I prefer people who are less serious.'

Marigold, French Jealousy. 'You are being unreasonable with your jealousy.'

Marjoram Modesty. 'Your forwardness makes me blush.'

Meadowsweet Uselessness. 'I want someone who is more than just good looking.'

Mimosa Sensitiveness. 'You are too brusque.'

Mint Homeliness. 'Look for someone your own age who is more suitable.'

Mistletoe Kisses. 'I send you a thousand kisses.'

Mock orange Cancelled wedding. 'I no longer wish to marry you.'

71

Moneywort   Fidelity. 'I am forever yours.'

Morning glory   Affection. 'I think a great deal of you.'

Mullein   Friendship. 'Let's be friends.'

Musk   Overadornment. 'Why not let your natural beauty shine through?'

Myrtle   Fragrance. 'Be my love.'

Narcissus   Self-love. 'You cannot love anyone while you love yourself so much.'

Nasturtium   Cunning. 'Be yourself. Stop trying to be so clever.'

Nemophilia   Prosperity. 'Congratulations on your success.'

Oak leaves   Courage. 'Don't give up for true love always finds a way.'

Oleander   Warning. 'Someone has betrayed our secret.'

Orchid   Luxury. 'I will make you truly happy. You will want for nothing.'

Pansy, purple   Souvenirs. 'These flowers remind me of happy times together.'

Pansy, white   Thoughts of love. 'You are always in my thoughts.'

Pansy, yellow   Remembrance. 'Even though we are apart, my thoughts are with you.'

Pasque flower   Denial. 'I have put aside material thoughts, to concentrate on the spiritual things of life. You are thus wasting your time.'

Passionflower   Refusal. 'I am promised elsewhere, but if you wish to wait, that is your decision.'

Pelargonium   Friendship. 'If you stop talking about love, I will be your friend.'

Peony   Contrition. 'I am sorry I was so off-hand with you.'

Periwinkle   First love. 'You have stolen my heart.'

Petunia   Closeness. 'When you are near me, I feel content.'

Phlox, pink   Friendship. 'I think we might be friends.'

Phlox, white   Interest. 'Tell me something about yourself.'

Pimpernel   Meeting. 'When and where can we get together? Can it be today please?'

Pink, clove   Fragrance. 'You are gorgeous.'

Poppy, red   Moderation. 'Stop being so pushy and take your time with me. Be patient.'

Poppy, white   Indecision. 'I have not made up my mind.'

Primrose   Dawning love. 'I might come to love you.'

Rhododendron   Danger. 'There are problems ahead. Take care.'
Rose, Christmas   Anxiety. 'Please let me know, one way or the other. I can't stand to wait much longer.'
Rose, moss   Shy love. 'I need to think about this from a distance. Let me do so.'
Rose, red   Love. 'I love you with all my heart.'
Rose, white   Refusal. 'I don't love you.'
Rose, yellow   Misplaced affection. 'I love someone else.'
Rosemary   Remembrance. 'I will never forget you, or you me.'
Salvia, red   Passion. 'Don't let the fire in our hearts burn out too quickly.'
Saxifrage   Humility. 'Just a smile from you keeps me alive.'
Snapdragon   Refusal. 'You mean nothing to me.'
Snowdrop   Renewal. 'I am trying again to see if you will ever love me.'
Solomon's seal   Simplicity. 'I am nothing, but I love you.'
Sunflower   Showiness. 'I am not impressed by showy, outward appearances.'
Sweetpea   Tenderness. 'I think of you with affection.'
Sweet William   Fun. 'I was only teasing you.'
Tansy   Rejection. 'I am not interested in you.'
Thrift   Interest. 'Tell me more about yourself.'
Thyme   Domesticity. 'I need a wife as capable as you are.'
Toadflax   Reluctance. 'You must back off and be less hasty.'
Trumpetflower   Passion. 'I burn with desire for you.'
Tuberose   Wounding. 'You have changed me. This is getting too dangerous.'
Tulip, red   Avowal. 'With this flower, I declare my love for you.'
Tulip, yellow   Refusal. 'Your love is hopeless.'
Valerian   Love. 'I have little to offer you but I would like to marry you.'
Verbena   Enthralment. 'You must pray for me, because I am lost in love to you.'
Veronica   True love. 'Nothing will ever part us.'
Violet   Modesty. 'You are pure and sweet.'
Wallflower   Constancy. 'I am true to you, no matter what.'
Woodbine   Affection. 'I love you and am always your friend.'
Wormwood   Parting. 'Best of friends, we must part.'

Having become acquainted with the meanings of the flowers, it might have been necessary to send a message giving a specific time for meeting. The Victorians had thought of this, and also had a lover's floral clock. Ivy meant that you wished to meet. So by placing another flower with the ivy, you could state whether you meant morning or afternoon, or even tomorrow, and with the floral clock you could also say at what time, although one had to be certain on the place, and as the 24-hour clock was not used, what part of the day the sender meant. As we have learnt, ivy meant 'meet me'. We have also discovered that white campion meant 'evening'. Consequently, a little tribute of ivy and white campion would mean 'meet me this evening'. If you added one of the flowers listed below, you would also learn precisely what time. If you wanted to make the meeting in the morning, obviously, you would use the bellflower, which means 'morning'. If you wished to reply, you could send ivy and white clover, which is about meeting someone and also about being true to your lover.

Flower	Time
Carnation	12 o'clock
Red rose	1 o'clock
Marjoram	2 o'clock
Violet	3 o'clock
Field daisy	4 o'clock
Sweetpea	5 o'clock
Broom	6 o'clock
Sweet William	7 o'clock
Jonquil	8 o'clock
Herb Robert	9 o'clock
Clove pink	10 o'clock
Sweet sultan	11 o'clock

In addition to the flowers listed above, the following special combinations were used for specific circumstances. Obviously, if there were flowers which had a special meaning and were a secret code between the couple themselves, these would be used as a preference, so what follows is merely a guideline, based on what we have already discussed:

74

- Ivy and lavender – 'I cannot meet you.'
- Ivy and red clover – 'I will meet you, but we will have to make another appointment.'
- Ivy and buttercup – 'I will meet you tomorrow, but cannot see you before.'

So, for example, if a young man wished to meet a young lady at 10 o'clock, as it was unlikely that she would go out on her own in the evening, it would be assumed to be a morning meeting. She would therefore receive a gift of ivy and clove pink, perhaps also with bellflowers, indicating a morning meeting, if he felt that needed underlining. If he wanted to make her aware of his affections, he could also include within the bouquet balsam or red carnation, or if this were only the start of the relationship, he might consider something like white hyacinth or white pansy as part of the gift. If he, by return, received a single white deadnettle, he would immediately know that he was wasting his time, and that he need not turn up for the appointment. If, however, he received a begonia, that would indicate that his young lady felt that they were being watched, so maybe another appointment should be made.

There are many combinations for all sorts of messages – you might wish to try some for yourself. It is interesting and a challenge, not only finding the right message, but also making an attractive bouquet of the flowers as well!

Dreaming of Flowers

It is rare that a dream revolves totally around just a flower, unless the dreamer works with flowers on a day-to-day basis. More often than not, there are many factors making up the dream, and we really should look at the whole dream, rather than dissect it and try to find a meaning based on fragments. However, if you have had a dream about a flower, receiving a bouquet or something similar, you may wish to know what the traditional meanings of these dreams are. This is only a brief list, and those interested in the interpretation

of dreams should consult a book especially dedicated to this subject, such as *Dream Interpretation for beginners* in this series.

Acacia   Your hopes and passion will be realised.

Almond blossom   A happy home life.

Apple blossom   Good news will reach you soon.

Aster   Happiness and the end to your problems.

Balm   Illness which will be short lived.

Buttercups   Look at your problems rationally and use opportunities that come up.

Camellias   Intense happiness, albeit short lived.

Cherry tree   Hard work ahead.

Chrysanthemum   Increase in your social life (if picked). If received, increase in status due to helpful friends in business.

Clover   Follow advice given by others as you cannot fail to win through. Success.

Crocus   New things are on the horizon. Forget the past and get moving onwards.

Cypress   News about someone close or dear to you.

Daffodils   Forget your problems. They are past. You will be happy and successful.

Dahlia   Your affairs will improve and your ambitions will be achieved.

Daisy   A birth.

Evergreens   Any evergreen plant suggests lasting happiness, love and success.

Ferns   Success after hard work, unless the ferns are wilting, in which case problems are likely.

Forsythia   Happiness and peace of mind, and a happy new love affair.

Fuchsia   Try to relax and stop getting so tense.

Geranium   Change and new contacts. Unexpected wealth.

Gladiolus   Improvement within your job.

Goldenrod   Don't interfere in the affairs of others.

Harebell   True love.

Hawthorn   Better things to come.

Heather, white   Good luck. In fact, any colour heather indicates good fortune.

Heliotrope   A quiet but satisfying life, with a modest but secure future.

Holly   Disappointments or problems are on the way, especially if it prickled you.

Honeysuckle   Love, happiness and new opportunities.

Hyacinth   Improvement through unexpected sources.

Iris   Contentment and prosperity.

Ivy   Faithfulness and tenacity. This shows success in everything, and happiness.

Jasmine   Romance.

Jessamine   Everything you could wish for is indicated here.

Laurel   Victory, prosperity and a happy marriage.

Lavender   Reunion with someone of the opposite sex.

Leaves   Happy marriage (if green), but difficulty or illness if dried up.

Lilac   Friendship.

Lily, Easter   Sudden rise in status.

Lily, red   You have desires to be wealthy.

Lily, white   You stand alone in your endeavours but are happy.

Marigold   Happiness in marriage and a faithful lover. Success in all avenues of life.

Mistletoe   Patience required before you get what you want.

Myrtle   Gentle love, happiness to the single person and a large family.

Nasturtium   An unusual sexual experience is likely.

Nettles   You aren't in control of your life. Watch other people and their motives.

Orange blossom   A wedding is likely.

Orchid   You have faithful and loving friends, and have much to be happy about, but watch your spending.

Parsley   Success. You will get some lucky opportunities. Take them.

Passion flower   Separation.

Peony   Anxiety.

Petunia   A good social life (if outside), but if inside, this indicates boredom.

Pinks   Good times with good company.

Poppy, red   Happiness, and maybe a romance, if the poppies are picked. Watch your passions.

Poppy, yellow   Sensual delight.

Rose

Rose, red   Love and happiness. Picking a rose, of any colour, indicates new friends and possibly new love.
Rosemary   Reunion.
Sage   Advancement through wisdom and discretion.
Sunflower   Don't be impulsive, and don't trust new acquaintances.
Thyme   A happy marriage and prosperity.
Tulip, red   Secret marriage or romance.
Tulip, white   Problems at work.
Violet   Love, if the violet is in season at the time of the dream. Otherwise success in business and fame and fortune.
Wallflower   A secret admirer.
Water lilies   Things are out of reach. Readjust your goals.
Willow   Don't trust a new friend. Good news of an old friend.
Wormwood   Disappointments.
Yew   Money from unexpected sources.
Yucca   If in bloom, material and spiritual happiness will be yours.

Flowers generally in a dream are taken to be good signs, but these may be short lived, in much the same way as the flower itself withers and dies eventually, despite care and attention. Herbs also are a good sign generally, unless the herb is associated with poisons, such as hemlock, henbane, etc., in which case danger is suggested.

Other flower symbolism might be:

- Making up a bouquet means a marriage.
- Receiving a bouquet shows you have friends.
- Arranging flowers indicates improvements in your life.
- Vases of flowers mean good times to come, with financial improvements.
- Picking flowers indicates good fortune.
- Dried flowers indicate obstacles or illnesses.
- Artificial flowers indicate a pressured situation where you could go against your better judgement.
- Wild flowers indicate an adventure.
- Throwing away flowers indicates quarrels.
- Dropping either a flower or petal indicates thoughtlessness which will result in personal unhappiness.
- Flowers in a meadow means your partner loves you as much as you love him or her.
- A flower garden means love and companionship, but if it is unkempt it indicates difficulties in the future or confusion at present.
- Falling petals indicate a parting.
- Bushes, either fighting though them or seeing them in a garden indicate changes.
- Plants, if flowering, suggest unexpected things in the near future.
- Dried or dying plants suggest you need to sort out a misunderstanding.

*　　*　　*

In this chapter, we have looked at the hidden meanings behind flowers, both to the Victorians and in dream state. In Chapter 6, we will be taking a further look at the symbolism of flowers.

5
WILD FLOWERS, HERBS AND THEIR POWERS

*Y*ou may be interested in making part of your garden a herbal area, but you are not sure where to start. My advice is to take the bull by the horns. Even those people who live in a flat can create a small herb garden, using pots. Most herbs do well in pots; bay, parsley, mint and chives do especially well. Thyme also grows well in pots, takes up little space and makes a good gargle for coughs and colds. Some people consider that a herb garden without thyme is not a herb garden at all!

The first thing to do is to decide for yourself which herbs you would like to grow. You may wish to think about creating a planetary herbal garden.

PLANETARY HERBS

People who have an interest in the planets may wish to make a planetary herbal garden, using all, or only a selection, of the herbs listed below.

You will notice that some herbs relate to more than one planet. I have also given details on trees and fruits which correspond to the planets according to tradition, should you wish to organise the whole of your garden around a planetary theme.

Sun   Marigold, bay tree, borage, rosemary, angelica, rue, sorrel, fennel, St John's wort and camomile. Other herbs or spices should connect with the element of Fire, such as cinnamon, clove and patchouli. Citrus fruits such as oranges relate to the sun, and in warmer climes this might be something to consider. Likewise, the vine and ash tree, bay, juniper and walnut connect with the sun.

Moon   Hyssop, mistletoe, rosemary, lemon balm, saxifrage, clary, honeysuckle, chives, comfrey and witch hazel. Lettuce and cucumber also connect with the moon because of their high water content, as do watercress, water caltrops and lotus. Trees which connect with the moon include olive, palm, willow, privet and maple.

Mercury   Fennel, valerian, summer savory, mulberry, balsam, marjoram, oregano, caraway, southern wood, calamint, lavender, horehound, dill, red clover, vervain, comfrey, meadowsweet, tansy and parsley. Trees which connect to Mercury include hazel, mulberry, myrtle and the pomegranate.

Venus   Sage, clover, sorrel, yarrow, thyme, lovage, burdock, celandine, daffodils (not yellow as these belong to Mars), peppermint, heather, dandelion, primrose, cowslip pennyroyal and golden samphire. In the fruit realm, apples, plums, figs and strawberries also connect to Venus, as do alder, almond, apricot, blackberry, cherry, gooseberry, peach, pear, poplar, raspberry and sycamore. The laurel, birch and rowan trees are also connected to Venus.

Mars   Sweet basil, tarragon, hops, blue flags, mustard, chives, soapwort, wormwood, garlic, yellow daffodils, gentian, ginger,

marjoram, horseradish, pulsatilla and valerian. Peppers and onions also relate to Mars, as do nettles, box, broom, hawthorn and thistles. The pine tree also connects with Mars.

Jupiter   Sage, agrimony, balm, borage, hyssop, mint, dock, chicory, marjoram and chervil. In trees, the oak, ash and fir tree connect with Jupiter. Trees which connect are normally perennials, such as date, fir, oak, lime and fig. Some would suggest that as Jupiter is concerned with justice, the hyssop also links.

Saturn   Comfrey, quince, Solomon's seal, (used to take the colour out of bruises), viola tricolour, mullein, henbane, ivy, monkshood, nightshade, helleborus niger (Christmas rose) and elder. The yew and yucca are also connected, as are beech, cypress, poplar, sloe, service tree, tamarisk and buckthorn. Eucalyptus also connects, as does holly and horse chestnut.

Uranus   Tansy, valerian, fumitory and horehound.

Neptune   Meadowsweet, woodruff, burnet, lungwort, verbain, camomile, hart's tongue, liver wort, saxifrage and peppermint.

You may wish to assign only one particular planetary link to your herb garden, based on your own astrological symbol and the planet to which it relates. For those who are unsure of their links, these are given below.

Aries   21 March to 20 April – ruled by Mars.
Taurus   21 April to 21 May – ruled by Venus.
Gemini   22 May to 21 June – ruled by Mercury.
Cancer   22 June to 23 July – ruled by the Moon.
Leo   24 July to 23 August – ruled by the Sun.
Virgo   24 August to 23 September – ruled by Mercury.
Libra   24 September to 23 October – ruled by Venus.
Scorpio   24 October to 22 November – ruled by Pluto but also associated with Mars.
Sagittarius   23 November to 21 December – ruled by Jupiter.
Capricorn   22 December to 20 January – ruled by Saturn.
Aquarius   21 January to 19 February – ruled by both Uranus and Saturn.
Pisces   20 February to 20 March – ruled by Neptune.

Conversely, if you have your full natal chart (a chart drawn up by an astrologer giving all the planets associated with you from the details given of your date and place of birth), you may wish to assign all the planets to your herbal garden.

Looking at the links we have already established between colour, chakras, herbs and days, you can really have some fun creating a totally individual herbal plot, using all the information we have discovered. For example, if you were born on a Tuesday, the herb you could consider would be urtica, with your main colour red. Linking this with Mars, the planet normally associated with red, you could also then link the herbs and flowers discussed above, especially if you were also an Aries by zodiac sign. Really, there is no end to the fun you could have creating a garden around such a theme.

LINKING WITH FENG SHUI

Those people who haven't heard of this term may like to know that it is an ancient Chinese art of management of positive forces for beneficial effect, and literally means 'wind and water'. Concerned with making our environment harmonious, it dates back at least 5,000 years and concerns both our living accommodation, our work environment and our overall health. Even placing a plant or single flower in an ill-advised position can alter the harmony of a room, and it is felt by the Chinese especially, that the harmony created by ideal Feng Shui situations will help with prosperity, health and good fortune. Feng Shui is a very detailed subject, and *Feng Shui for beginners*, another book in this series, will give you complete details of this art, and open up many interesting avenues for you to consider where plants, flowers, herbs and gardens can play an active part.

Within the framework of gardens, flowers, plants and herbs, you can, if you so wish, create a beneficial harmony within the garden, creating a positive balance of ch'i (natural energy), and thus creating harmony for yourself and your family and friends. Thinking in terms

of ch'i as an active force moving around a home, it is necessary to consider its movement, how it comes in and leaves through windows and doors, can be diverted by mirrors and flows in gentle curves around one's environment. One important part of Feng Shui concerns the placement of plants and flowers, and it is felt, for example, that the placing of plants in a bathroom draws vitality away from the environment, and creates disharmony.

As Feng Shui is concerned with the pathway of ch'i energies, a garden designed specifically to create a balance between the positive and negative can be created easily. Most gardens designed around the principles of Feng Shui have winding paths, some water area, flower areas, trees and lawns. The Chinese consider a garden without any water to be devoid of life, and the insertion of a small pond with a fountain, if appropriate, can alter the whole garden and encourage the ch'i energies to circulate. Feng Shui also connects with the elements of wood, fire, earth, metal and water, and also with colours specifically attached to those elements. Wood is connected with blue and green, fire with red, earth with yellow, metal with white or silver-grey, and water with black or navy blue.

Growing Herbs

If you feel, however, that a standard herbal garden is your aim, do think about whether you may wish to use herbs for culinary purposes, beauty aims or from a health angle. Herbs are relatively easy to grow, and most people will at least be able to grow mint, parsley and perhaps garlic in their gardens without much difficulty. Remember, however, that mint does spread very quickly, and you may wish to create a barrier to stop it taking over the whole of the plot. A sprig of mint in potatoes adds a lovely taste to your vegetables, as well as helping with headaches, stress, insomnia and digestion problems.

Most herbs are available at garden centres, and you can always seek advice there on the best herbs for your soil and the location of your plot. In general, the best location is a sunny aspect, with moderately

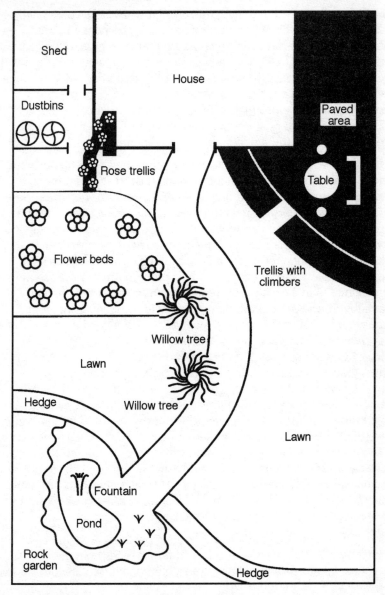

Garden designed to Feng Shui principles

fertile soil and good drainage. I always grow my herbs organically, having a natural dislike of anything artificial or chemical, but I do feed my herbs with garden compost from time to time, taking care not to overfeed. If you have a wall or hedge area where the sun will reach, you may wish to use this for your herb garden. My own area is a small box-shape bordered by a lawn, a hedge, a wall and a path. Try spacing your plants about 45 cm (18 inches) apart, and take care that you position the larger plants at the rear of the plot, so as not to cast too much shade on the smaller herbs.

If you feel you really aren't into herbs, other than from an aesthetic angle, you can at least consider planting nasturtiums, lavender, marigolds and feverfew, all of which can be used for health purposes. Nasturtiums are easily grown from seed, have leaves which can be used in salads, being rich in vitamin C, and help with breathing problems of a minor nature. You can also try using the dried seeds of the nasturtium in ground form as seasoning on food. Lavender is always a lovely sight, especially when properly trimmed. You can either buy plants or take cuttings, and putting a couple of sprigs of lavender in the bath or inhaling it can help those suffering from stress and tension to unwind. Lavender is also a good antiseptic, and lavender essential oil is one of the main items in an aromatherapy first-aid kit, being useful in most circumstances, but especially on cuts, grazes and burns. Marigolds can be grown in pots, or placed into the garden area, can be grown from seed, plant, cuttings or from root divisions from existing plants. Great for colds, indigestion and breathing difficulties, they prefer a warm, dry soil and are also very useful in the treatment of cuts and abrasions. Used as an infusion (15 g (0.5 oz) of fresh or dried marigold flowers to 200 ml (7 fl. oz) of boiling water), used as a wash or tincture, many types of wound can be effectively treated. Feverfew is great for migraines and headaches, and forms a nice addition to any border area. Most garden centres will have feverfew plants available for purchase.

You may also wish to think about creating a natural area, full of wild flowers – it is now possible to buy wild-flower seeds from many commercial outlets – and thus create a natural area within your garden.

Astrological affinities

Those people interested in astrology may wish to know which plants and flowers link naturally with them.

Aries   Anemone, basil, briony, coriander, cress, crow's foot, flaxweed, garlic, ginger, honeysuckle, mustard, onions, peppers and any trees with thorns.

Taurus   Almond, apricot, ash, cloves, colt's foot, cowslip, elder flowers, ferns, grape, groundsel, lily, lovage, mint, primrose, red cherry, sorrel, tansy, thyme and violets.

Taurus people make good gardeners, will normally enjoy gardening and be good at flower arrangements and anything involving interior design.

Gemini   Carrot, cress, dill, garlic, haresfoot, hogweed, lavender, mandrake, mulberry and parsley.

Cancer   Cabbage, cardamine, chickweed, flax, maple, mushroom, olive, pumpkin, saxifrage, turnip and white rose.

Cancer people like plants, especially receiving potted plants and flowers and gifts. They also like sending flowers to people.

Leo   Almond, angelica, bay, celandine, camomile, frankincense, juniper, lemon, marigold, mistletoe, orange, rosemary and saffron.

Virgo   Azalea, balm, caraway, fenugreek, endive, fennel, hazel, lily-of-the-valley, marjoram, myrtle, sage, savory and valerian.

Virgos make exceptional gardeners in the main and will enjoy time spent in the garden.

Libra   Apple, artichoke, chestnut, daffodil, daisy, foxglove, groundsel, lily, mint, parsley, pennyroyal, rose and yarrow.

Libra people like flowers and like arranging flowers. Liking things well balanced, their gardens will normally be well thought through and designed.

Scorpio   Aloes, briar, broom, cactus, furze, garlic, leeks, nettles, radish and thistle.

Sagittarius   Almond, ash, borage, chervil, cloves, dandelion, mint, myrrh, sage and tomato.

Capricorn   Barley, beech, beet, burdock, comfrey, cypress, deadly nightshade, elm, hemlock, holly, ivy, spinach, willow and yew. Connecting with the earth, Capricorn people usually make good gardeners.

Aquarius   Comfrey, golden-rain, heartsease, hemp, mandrake, moss, pansies, parsnips, pine, quince, rushes and sorrel.

Pisces   Aniseed, balm, birch, chestnut, daisy, dandelion, dock, kelp, marjoram, nutmeg, oak, sage, strawberry and water lily.

fLOWER SYMBOLISM

6

*A*s with any form of symbolism, flowers can hold a personal
meaning for one person which is not shared with others, or
perhaps is shared between two people for whom a particular
flower or plant holds a special significance or memory. In this
chapter, we are going to take a brief look at some flower
symbolism, including looking at the symbolism of our first names
from a flower angle. Names in themselves are symbols, and often
this link seems to be missed.

LOOKING AT fLOWERS

The symbolism of flowers can involve both the flower itself, and the
shape of the flower, the number of its petals, leaves, etc. Here we
are going to deal only with the meaning of flowers themselves,
leaving the shape issue to further study.

Generally, flowers are symbolic of growth, springtime and beauty.
Many centuries ago, amazed at the power of the sun to provide heat
and light, ancient peoples linked things of a yellow or golden colour
with what they felt to be the magical powers of the sun. One of these
flowers is the **sunflower**, which was thought to strengthen the mind
and bring about an increase in energy, in much the same way as the
sun itself was seen to give energy to flowers and plants, and increase
their growth. Alchemists felt that the flower was symbolic of the work
of the sun, and they gave the name 'celestial flower' to a comet or

shooting star. The colour of the flowers was also important. Obviously anything remotely yellow coloured represented the sun, while red flowers symbolised life (blood is red) and passion, and so on.

Gardens themselves, symbolic of consciousness (gardens are normally planned, whereas in the world of nature this is not the case – as forests are symbolic of the unconscious), are given a feminine principle in the main, although many gardeners and especially famous landscape gardeners tend to be men.

Many flowers were felt to be home to evil spirits, and various flowers were connected with spirits, elves, fairies and sprites as we have seen in Chapter 3.

Connected with the heart and with love, the **rose** linked with Venus, Aphrodite, Ishtar and Isis, and became a symbol of virginity, martydom and love. Linked to a search for spirituality and perfection, the original symbol of love was the red tulip, but only in parts of Europe does this link remain. To most lovers, the red rose is the true symbol of love, and for this reason, many cards and gifts have, as their symbol, the red rose. Lovers through the centuries have sent and received red roses, with a single red rose being thought of as completion and perfection. Should a person therefore receive such a gift, it is a symbol of the sender's affection and his or her feelings of being complete and of the receiver being the perfect mate. It was also felt that sleeping with rose petals under your pillow at night would bring about dreams of a future lover.

To students of the Qabalah, the rose links to Tiphareth, and is symbolic of beauty and harmony. Because of its links with ancient religions and traditions, the rose was shunned by the early Christian Church. However, with the possible aim of trying to convert heathens and pagans to believe in Christianity, the Church eventually linked the rose to the Virgin Mary, seeking to link her to the earlier pagan goddesses in the minds of those whom the Church was trying to convert. At one time, it is said that rosary beads were made from rose petals, hence the name.

The rose was dedicated to Harpocrates, god of Silence, and it was once believed that anything said in a room containing a ceiling decoration of roses would remain secret. This thought was behind

the naming of taverns, and the Romans actively sought out places where a rose was displayed outside, as it signified that anything said inside, whether in a state of sobriety or drunkenness, would remain totally confidential. The colours of the rose are quite symbolic. To the Romans, white and red roses were often planted on the tombs of dead lovers, white symbolising modesty and red symbolising passion. Blue roses are symbolic of impossibility, while the yellow rose is a symbol of achievement and wisdom.

Pansies are symbolic of thought, and their five petals are symbolic of man himself. Pansies are one of the flowers mentioned by Shakespeare in *Hamlet* ('There's rosemary, that's for remembrance . . . and there is pansies, that's for thoughts'). The **narcissus** on the other hand is named after a person, a Greek young man of the same name who was told that he would have a happy life unless he saw his image reflected. Unfortunately, he caught sight of his reflection in a stream, and legend tells that he fell desperately in love with himself, and unable to move away from the stream, slowly died. Linking this flower with the legend, leads the narcissus to be symbolic of love, of self and of others, and the enrichment of relationships. It can also, however, be symbolic of introspection and a self-sufficient attitude.

Lilies are symbolic of purity, and often linked to the Virgin Mary. Said also to connect to the fleur-de-lis, the lily was once a sign of royalty, but more commonly, lilies represent purity. Within the Bible, the term lily probably also covers other flowers, and where mention is made of the lilies of the field and their beauty, some scholars suggest that the actual flower being mentioned was the **anemone**, which is symbolic of the wind, as it connects with the Greek nymph who was pursued by the wind and changed into the anemone flower.

Hyacinth is a flower symbolic of all the meanings of the colour purple, from royalty through to spirituality, and was so called, legend suggests, after a girl of the same name who left a memory of colour and perfume.

The **iris** is symbolic of love especially within the United States, where its root is still sometimes sprinkled on to the sheets of a bed in order to arouse passionate feelings. Said to bring about a link between the conscious and unconscious mind, it is also thought to

link the material with the spiritual, heaven with earth. Iris is also the name of the messenger of the gods, who took the form of a rainbow, which itself is also seen to link heaven to earth, and as such, irises can sometimes be symbolic of communication and messages.

The **jasmine** is a flower sacred to the Chinese, and is symbolic of femininity and purity, and is said to induce feelings of physical attraction and sensuality. Considered to help men bring a new love into their lives and enable them to be more open about their feelings, it is also thought to help boost self-esteem and is often found in bridal bouquets.

Names as symbols

We are now going to take a brief look at the linking of flowers and the world of nature with names, with apologies to male readers, as men do not link to flowers and nature in the most part. This is not an exhaustive list, but is included to show the symbolic link and importance that we have placed on flowers and plants, even going so far as to link our children's names to the wonders of nature. It will come as little surprise to most readers to discover that many names have roots in the Greek language.

Amaryllis From the Greek, meaning 'rippling stream'.
Anthea From the Greek *anthos*, meaning 'a flower'.
Asta From the Greek *aster*, meaning 'starlike'.
Azalea From the Latin word meaning 'dry earth'. This plant thrives in such conditions.
Basil From the Greek word *basileios* meaning 'royal' rather than linking directly to the herb of the same name.
Blossom From the old English word *blostm* meaning fresh and lovely, and actively linked to flowers, especially the snowflower.
Carmel From the Hebrew word, meaning 'garden' or 'God's vineyard'. Mount Carmel is mentioned in the Bible.
Cerelia From the Latin meaning 'of the spring' and connecting with someone as fresh and spring flowers.

Cherry   A variant of the word 'charity' and not actually connecting with the tree or the blossom. As a result, the name means 'charitable'.

Clematis   From the Greek *klematis*, meaning 'vine' or 'brushwood'.

Cliantha   From the Greek *kleianthe*, meaning 'glory-flower' or 'flower from heaven'.

Clover   From the old English *cleafer*, meaning 'clover blossom'.

Clytie   From the Greek *klytai* which means 'splendid or beautiful one'. Legend suggests that Clytie was daughter of Oceanus, and was a nymph who was changed into a heliotrope flower because she loved the sun so much that she was always turning her face towards it.

Daffodil   From the old French word *afro-dille*. Said to have been touched by Pluto and turned to gold from white, the daffodil is symbolic of the springtime.

Dahlia   From the old Norse word *dal-r,* meaning 'from the valley'. This flower is actually named from the Latin form of the surname of the Swedish botanist linked to its development A Dahl.

Daisy   From the old English *daegeseage* meaning 'day's eye'. Thought by many to be a miniature replica of the sun and its rays, the French call this flower the **Marguerite**, and as such this is also a name linked to the daisy flower.

Delfine   From the Greek *delphinion* – the larkspur or delphinium flower, so named because the centre of the flower is thought to resemble a dophin.

Eglantine   From the old French word *aiglentine* meaning sweetbrier rose or woodbine.

Eranthe   From the Greek word *ear-anthemos* meaning 'spring flower'.

Fleur   French for 'flower', this name conjours up beautiful thoughts of flowers.

Flora   From the Latin word, Flora was the Roman goddess of flowers.

Gardenia   From the white flower of the same name, the plant actually gets its name from the eighteenth-century American botanist, Alexander Garden, someone who obviously had the right name for the occupation he chose!

Geranium   From the Greek *geranion* which actually means 'crane' and does not obviously link with the flower of the same name.

Hazel   From the old English *haesel*, this name links with the tree of the same name. Ancient peoples believed that the hazel branch signified rulership.

Heather   From the Middle English word *hadder* meaning 'as the heather'.

Holly   From the Old English words *holen* and *halig* relating to the bush of the same name.

Hortense   From the Latin word *hortensia* meaning 'of the garden'.

Iantha or **Iolanthe**   From the Greek *ianthinos* meaning 'violet-coloured flower'.

Iris   From the Greek, and meaning 'rainbow'.

Ivy   From the Old English *ifig* and named after the plant of the same name.

Jasmine   From the Persian, and meaning 'like the jasmine flower'.

Koren   From the Greek *kore* and linking to the lotus flower, this name means 'maiden'.

Lala   From the Slavic, meaning 'tulip flower'.

Laurel   Linking with Lauren, Loretta, Lorna and Laura, this name comes from the Latin *laurea*, which was a crown of laurel leaves, given as an emblem in victory.

Laverne   From the Old French *la vergne* meaning from the alder-tree or grove. This name also links to the Latin word *vernis* meaning springlike.

Lilac   From the Persian word *nilak*, this links with the story of a Persian girl who was known for her blue-black hair, in much the same way as the lilac can often have a bluish colour.

Lilian   From the Latin *lilium*, meaning like a lily. Other forms of this name are Lily, Lil, Liliane, Lilyan and Lilias. This name was popular early in the twentieth century.

Lotus   From the Greek *lotos* and linked to the flower venerated by many civilisations.

Magnolia   From the Latin word, and linking to the magnolia tree and flower. The magnolia tree was itself named after Pierre Magnol, the seventeenth-century French botanist.

Malva   From the Latin word meaning 'mallow flower'.

Marigold   From the English flower of the same name.

May   From the Roman goddess Maia, and resembling the May blossom.

Melantha   From the Greek word *melanthos* meaning 'dark flower'.

Minta   From the Greek meaning 'the mint plant'.

Myrtle   From the Greek *myrtos*, meaning 'like the myrtle'. Myrtle was the ancient Greek symbol of triumph and victory, much as the laurel was to the Romans.

Olive   From the Latin *olivia*, this name concerns the olive tree and olive branch, and is thus symbolic of peace.

Peony   From the Latin *Paeonia*, the god of healing. Sacred to Pan, the Greek god, and also to Apollo, this flower is much loved by many.

Petunia   From the Tupi Indian word *petum*, this links to the story of an Indian girl of the same name, as well as to the reddish-purple flower.

Philantha   From the Greek *philanthos*, meaning 'flower lover'.

Poppy   From the Latin word *papaver*, this name obviously links to the flower.

Primrose   From the Latin word *primula*, meaning little first one, this is one of the early flowers of the year.

Reseda   From the Latin word meaning 'mignonette flower'.

Rhodanthe   Also Rhoda, Rose, Rosanne, Rosalie, Rosalinda, Rosette and Rosina, this name links with the Greek word *rhodos* meaning 'a rose'.

Rosemary   From the English word for the plant of the same name, this name means 'rose of St Mary', and links with remembrance. Some scholars suggest that the root of the word 'Rosemary' comes from the Latin word *rosmarinus* meaning 'dew of the sea'.

Sadira   From the Persian word *sadar* meaning 'the lotus tree'.

Salvia   From the Latin word *salvia* meaning 'sage', the herb.

Spring   From the Old English *springan* meaning 'springtime'. This was once a very popular name.

Susan   From the Hebrew *shoshannah* meaning 'lily'.

Sylvia   From the Latin *silva* meaning 'of the forest', other names include Sylvester, Silvana and Silva.

Tamara   From the Hebrew *tamar* and linked to the palm tree.

Verbena   From the Latin *verbenae* meaning 'sacred boughs', verbena is more commonly now associated with the art of aromatherapy, and is the common name for a shrub found in Chile and Peru from which comes the oil used to aid digestive complaints.

Verna   From the Latin meaning 'springlike', legend tells of a spring nymph of the same name who dressed in green and wore bright flowers in her hair.

Violet   From the Old French word *violete* meaning 'violet flower'. Other names derived from this root form include Yolanda.

Zera   From the Herbrew *zera'im* meaning 'seeds'.

Zinnia   From the Latin word linked to the zinnia flower, so named after J G Zinn.

fURThER READING

fLOWERS AND pLANTS

Blacklock, Judith, *Teach Yourself Dried Flowers*, Hodder & Stoughton, 1993.
Blacklock, Judith, *Teach Yourself Flower Arranging*, Hodder & Stoughton, 1992.
Grigson, Geoffrey, *The Englishman's Flora*, London, 1960.
Kromdijk, G., *200 House Plants in Colour*, Lutterworth Press, 1969.
Nicholson, B. E., Ary, S., Gregory, M., *The Oxford Book of Wild Flowers*, Oxford University Press, 1973.
Savage, F. G., *The Flora and Folklore of Shakespeare*, London, 1923.
Thistleton Dyer, T. F., *The Folklore of Plants*, London, 1889.

Homoeopathy and herbalism

Culpeper, Nicholas, *The English Physician*, 1652.
Gibson, D. H., *First Aid Homoeopathy in Accidents and Ailments*, British Homoeopathic Association, 1982.
Gibson, Mrs Sheila and Robin, *Homoeopathy for Everyone*, Penguin.
Grieve, Mrs M., *A Modern Herbal*, 1932.
Griggs, Barbara, *Green Pharmacy*, Jill Norman and Hobhouse.
Locke, Dr Andrew, *The Family Guide to Homoeopathy*, Guild Publishing, 1989.
McIntyre, Anne, *Herbal Medicine*, Macdonald Optima, 1987.
Nightingale, Dr Micheal, *Holistic First Aid*, Macdonald Optima, 1988.

Wheater, Caroline, *Common Ailments Cured Naturally*, Ward Lock, 1991.
White, Susie, *Teach Yourself Herbs*, Hodder & Stoughton, 1993.

AROMATHERAPY

Brown, Denise, *Teach Yourself Aromatherapy*, Hodder & Stoughton, 1996.
Davis, Patricia, *Aromatherapy, an A–Z*, CW Daniel, 1988.
Metcalfe, Joannah, *Herbs and Aromatherapy*, Bloomsbury Books, 1989.
Tisserand, Robert, *The Art of Aromatherapy*, 1977.
Westwood, Christine, *Aromatherapy, A Guide for Home Use*, Kerbina, 1991.

COLOUR THERAPY

Wills, Pauline, *Colour Therapy*, Element, 1993.
Wills, Pauline, *Working With Colour – a beginner's guide*, Hodder & Stoughton, 1997.

MEDITATION

Enelow, Gertrude, *Body Dynamics*, Information Incorporated, New York, 1960.
Fontana, Dr D., *The Meditator's Handbook*, Element, 1992.
Hewitt, James, *Teach Yourself Meditation*, Hodder & Stoughton, 1992.
Hewitt, James, *Teach Yourself Relaxation*, Hodder & Stoughton, 1985.
Ozaniec, Naomi, *Meditation for beginners*, Hodder & Stoughton, 1995.
Ozaniec, Naomi, *Teach Yourself Meditation*, Hodder & Stoughton, 1997
Whitehill, James, *Enter the Quiet: Everyone's way to meditation*, Harper and Row, New York, 1980.
Wills, Pauline, *Teach Yourself Visualization*, Hodder & Stoughton, 1996.
Wills, Pauline, *Visualisation for beginners*, Hodder & Stoughton, 1995.

Titles in this series

Astral Projection 0 340 67418 0   £5.99   Is it possible for the soul to leave the body at will? In this book the traditional techniques used to achieve astral projection are described in a simple, practical way, and Out of the Body and Near Death Experiences are also explored.

Chakras 0 340 62082 X   £5.99   The body's energy centres, the chakras, can act as gateways to healing and increased self-knowledge. This book shows you how to work with chakras in safety and with confidence.

Chinese Horoscopes 0 340 64804 X   £5.99   In the Chinese system of horoscopes, the year of birth is all-important. *Chinese Horoscopes for beginners* tells you how to determine your own Chinese horoscope, what personality traits you are likely to have, and how your fortunes may fluctuate in years to come.

Dowsing 0 340 60882 X   £5.99   People all over the world have used dowsing since the earliest times. This book shows how to start dowsing – what to use, what to dowse, and what to expect when subtle energies are detected.

Dream Interpretation 0 340 60150 7   £5.99   This fascinating introduction to the art and science of dream interpretation explains how to unravel the meaning behind dream images to interpret your own and other people's dreams.

Feng Shui 0 340 62079 X   £5.99   This beginner's guide to the ancient art of luck management will show you how to increase your good fortune and well-being by harmonising your environment with the natural energies of the earth.

Gems and Crystals 0 340 60883 8   £5.99   For centuries gems and crystals have been used as an aid to healing and meditation. This guide tells you all you need to know about choosing, keeping and using stones to increase your personal awareness and improve your well-being.

The Goddess 0 340 68390 2   £5.99   This book traces the development, demise and rebirth of the Goddess, looking at the worship of Her and retelling myths from all over the world.

Graphology 0 340 60625 8   £5.99   Graphology, the science of interpreting handwriting to reveal personality, is now widely accepted and used throughout the world. This introduction will enable you to make a comprehensive analysis of your own and other people's handwriting to reveal the hidden self.

Herbs for Magic and Ritual 0 340 67415 6   £4.99   This book looks at the well-known herbs and the stories attached to them. There is information on the use of herbs in essential oils and incense, and on their healing and magical qualities.

I Ching 0 340 62080 3   £5.99   The roots of *I Ching* or the *Book of Changes* lie in the time of the feudal mandarin lords of China, but its traditional wisdom is still relevant today. Using the original poetry in its translated form, this introduction traces its history, survival and modern-day applications.

Interpreting Signs and Symbols 0 340 68827 0   £5.99   The history of signs and symbols is traced in this book from their roots to the modern age. It also examines the way psychiatry uses symbolism, and the significance of doodles.

Love Signs 0 340 64805 8   £5.99   This is a practical introduction to the astrology of romantic relationships. It explains the different roles played by each of the planets, focusing particularly on the position of the Moon at the time of birth.

Meditation 0 340 64835 X   £5.99   This beginner's guide gives simple, clear instructions to enable you to start meditating and benefiting from this ancient mental discipline immediately. The text is illustrated throughout by full-colour photographs and line drawings.

Mediumship 0 340 68009 1   £5.99   Whether you want to become a medium yourself, or simply understand what mediumship is about, this book will give you the grounding to undertake a journey of discovery into the spirit realms.

Numerology 0 340 59551 5   £5.99   Despite being scientifically based, numerology requires no great mathematical talents to understand. This introduction gives you all the information you will need to understand the significance of numbers in your everyday life.

Pagan Gods for Today's Man 0 340 69130 1   £5.99   Looking at ancient gods and old stories, this guide explores the social and psychological issues affecting the role of men today. In these pages men of all ages and persuasions can find inspiration.

Paganism 0 340 67013 4   £5.99   Pagans are true Nature worshippers who celebrate the cycles of life. This guide describes pagan festivals and rituals and takes a detailed look at the many forms of paganism practised today.

Palmistry 0 340 59552 3   £5.99   Palmistry is the oldest form of character reading still in use. This illustrated guide shows you exactly what to look for and how to interpret what you find.

Qabalah 0 340 67339 7   £5.99   The Qabalah is an ancient Jewish system of spiritual knowledge centred on the Tree of Life. This guide explains how it can be used in meditation and visualisation, and links it to the chakras, yoga, colour therapy, crystals, Tarot and numerology.

Runes 0 340 62081 1   £5.99   The power of the runes in healing and giving advice about relationships and life in general has been acknowledged since the time of the Vikings. This book shows how runes can be used in our technological age to increase personal awareness and stimulate individual growth.

Shamanism 0 340 68010 5   £5.99   Shamanic technique offers direct contact with Spirit, vivid self-knowledge and true kinship with plants, animals and the planet Earth. This book describes the shamanic way, the wisdom of the Medicine Wheel and power animals.

Spiritual Healing 0 340 67416 4   £5.99   All healing starts with self, and the Universal Power which makes this possible is available to everyone. In this book there are exercises, techniques and guidelines to follow which will enable you to heal yourself and others spiritually.

Star Signs 0 340 59553 1   £5.99   This detailed analysis looks at each of the star signs in turn and reveals how your star sign affects everything about you. This book shows you how to use this knowledge in your relationships and in everyday life.

Tantric Sexuality 0 340 68349 X £5.99 Tantric Buddhists use sex as a pleasurable path to enlightenment. This guide offers a radically different and exciting new dimension to sex, explaining practical techniques in a clear and simple way.

Tarot 0 340 59550 7 £5.99 Tarot cards have been used for many centuries. This guide gives advice on which sort to buy, where to get them and how to use them. The emphasis is on using the cards positively, as a tool for gaining self-knowledge, while exploring present and future possibilities.

The Moon and You 0 340 64836 8 £5.99 The phase of the Moon when you were born radically affects your personality. This book looks at nine lunar types – how they live, love, work and play, and provides simple tables to find out the phase of your birth.

Visualisation 0 340 65495 3 £5.99 This introduction to visualisation, a form of self-hypnosis widely used by Buddhists, will show you how to practise the basic techniques – to relieve stress, improve your health and increase your sense of personal well-being.

Witchcraft 0 340 67014 2 £5.99 This guide to the ancient religion based on Nature worship answers many of the questions and uncovers the myths and misconceptions surrounding witchcraft. Mystical rituals and magic are explained and there is advice for the beginner on how to celebrate the Sabbats.

Working With Colour 0 340 67011 8 £5.99 Colour is the medicine of the future. This book explores the energy of each colour and its significance, gives advice on how colour can enhance our well-being, and gives ideas on using colour in the home and garden.

Your Psychic Powers 0 340 67417 2 £5.99 Are you psychic? This book will help you find out by encouraging you to look more deeply within yourself. Psychic phenomena such as precognitive dreams, out of body travels and visits from the dead are also discussed in this ideal stepping stone towards a more aware you.

To order this series

All books in this series are available from bookshops or, in case of difficulty, can be ordered direct from the publisher. Prices and availability subject to change without notice. Send your order with your name and address to : Hodder & Stoughton Ltd, Cash Sales Department, Bookpoint, 39 Milton Park, Abingdon, OXON, OX14 4TD, UK. If you have a credit card you may order by telephone – 01235 831700.

Please enclose a cheque or postal order made payable to Bookpoint Ltd, allow the following for postage and packing: UK & BFPO: £1.00 for the first book, 50p for the second book and 30p for each additional book ordered up to a maximum charge of £3.00. OVERSEAS & EIRE: £2.00 for the first book, £1.00 for the second book and 50p for each additional book.

For sales in the following countries please contact:
UNITED STATES: Trafalgar Square (Vermont), Tel: 800 423 4525 (toll-free)
CANADA: General Publishing (Ontario), Tel: 445 3333
AUSTRALIA: Hodder & Stoughton (Sydney), Tel: 02 638 5299